The Scientific Revolution

A Brief History with Documents

D0047960

Related Titles in
THE BEDFORD SERIES IN HISTORY AND CULTURE
Advisory Editors: Lynn Hunt, *University of California, Los Angeles*
David W. Blight, *Yale University*
Bonnie G. Smith, *Rutgers University*
Natalie Zemon Davis, *Princeton University*
Ernest R. May, *Harvard University*

The Scientific Revolution
A Brief History with Documents

Margaret C. Jacob
University of California, Los Angeles

BEDFORD/ST. MARTIN'S   Boston ♦ New York

For Bedford/St. Martin's

Publisher for History: Mary V. Dougherty
Director of Development for History: Jane Knetzger
Senior Editor: Heidi L. Hood
Developmental Editor: Kathryn Abbott
Editorial Assistant: Jennifer Jovin
Assistant Production Manager: Joe Ford
Production Assistant: Ashley Chalmers
Executive Marketing Manager: Jenna Bookin Barry
Project Management: Books By Design, Inc.
Index: Books By Design, Inc.
Text Design: Claire Seng-Niemoeller
Cover Design: Joy Lin
Cover Art: Movement of the Earth in Relation to the Sun, Facsimile of Harmonica by
  Andrea Cellarius, Amsterdam, 1660. The Art Archive/Bibliothèque des Arts
  Décoratifs/Gianni Dagli Orti.
Composition: TexTech International
Printing and Binding: RR Donnelley & Sons Company

President: Joan E. Feinberg
Editorial Director: Denise B. Wydra
Editor in Chief: Karen S. Henry
Director of Marketing: Karen R. Soeltz
Director of Editing, Design, and Production: Marcia Cohen
Assistant Director of Editing, Design, and Production: Elise S. Kaiser
Manager, Publishing Services: Emily Berleth

Library of Congress Control Number: 2009928647

Manufactured in the United States of America.

7   6   5   4   3
h   g   f   e   d

For information, write: Bedford/St. Martin's, 75 Arlington Street,
Boston, MA 02116   (617-399-4000)

ISBN-10: 0-312-65349-2
ISBN-13: 978-0-312-65349-1

Acknowledgments

Document 1: Nicolaus Copernicus, *On the Revolutions of the Heavenly Orbs.* Translated
by John F. Dobson and Selig Brodetsky. Occasional Notes, Royal Astronomical Society
No. 10, May 1947. Courtesy of the Royal Astronomical Society.
Document 6: *Discourse on Method.* Translation © Margaret C. Jacob and Bedford/
St. Martin's.

Distributed outside North America by PALGRAVE MACMILLAN.

Foreword

The Bedford Series in History and Culture is designed so that readers can study the past as historians do.

The historian's first task is finding the evidence. Documents, letters, memoirs, interviews, pictures, movies, novels, or poems can provide facts and clues. Then the historian questions and compares the sources. There is more to do than in a courtroom, for hearsay evidence is welcome, and the historian is usually looking for answers beyond act and motive. Different views of an event may be as important as a single verdict. How a story is told may yield as much information as what it says.

Along the way the historian seeks help from other historians and perhaps from specialists in other disciplines. Finally, it is time to write, to decide on an interpretation and how to arrange the evidence for readers.

Each book in this series contains an important historical document or group of documents, each document a witness from the past and open to interpretation in different ways. The documents are combined with some element of historical narrative—an introduction or a biographical essay, for example—that provides students with an analysis of the primary source material and important background information about the world in which it was produced.

Each book in the series focuses on a specific topic within a specific historical period. Each provides a basis for lively thought and discussion about several aspects of the topic and the historian's role. Each is short enough (and inexpensive enough) to be a reasonable one-week assignment in a college course. Whether as classroom or personal reading, each book in the series provides firsthand experience of the challenge—and fun—of discovering, recreating, and interpreting the past.

Lynn Hunt
David W. Blight
Bonnie G. Smith
Natalie Zemon Davis
Ernest R. May

Preface

Every aspect of life in our globally connected world has been profoundly shaped by science. We understand the content of food by reference to chemistry and calories; we regulate human reproduction often by recourse to chemicals; we appeal to a scientific understanding of the human body to ensure health and longevity; and, not least, we make war scientifically as well as technologically. None of this would be possible if not for the Scientific Revolution of the sixteenth through the eighteenth centuries. Despite the general understanding of the world-altering significance of the Scientific Revolution, the average instructor is hard pressed to find a book that combines a concise yet thorough introduction with relevant documents for use in a survey class. This book provides students and instructors with a unique volume that combines a scholarly yet accessible introduction with a collection of wide-ranging documents that illuminate the scientific work done in astronomy, physics, mechanical philosophy, scientific method, biology, and medicine, while also paying attention to the public controversies over and eventual acceptance of the new science.

The introduction in Part One reveals that before nature could be understood in new ways, certain basic philosophical concepts had to be put in place—atoms, mechanical action, and experimental techniques, just to name a few. For these new concepts to be accepted, old ideas and philosophies—in particular the ideas of Aristotle, Ptolemy, and their largely clerical supporters—had to be discarded. This struggle to put in place a new understanding of nature began with Nicolaus Copernicus (1473–1543) and culminated in the spectacular discoveries of Isaac Newton (1642–1727). Yet, even after Newton's death, it remained for future generations to build on and popularize the new science. In the process, people were arrested and imprisoned, books were banned, and careers were ruined—such was the nature of the struggle.

The documents in Part Two provide some of the foundational texts that put in place what is now accepted as a scientific understanding of the natural world, in particular physical entities and the human body. The documents represent the many facets of the new science, including works in astronomy, physics, mechanical philosophy, scientific method, biology, and medicine. Organized chronologically, they illustrate the steps along the way to the transformation of science: the belief that knowledge is progressive and the modern is better than the ancient; the increasingly achievable goal of relieving human suffering through experiment and medicine; the uniformity of all matter whether on earth or in the heavens; the rational self and not dogma as the arbiter of truth; the virtue of careful and painstaking observation, recording, and illustration for the use of others; and the application of mathematics to movement and change.

Aids for student learning are included throughout this volume. Document headnotes and gloss notes provide students with the context for understanding each actor in the drama that was the Scientific Revolution. The illustrations that are interspersed in the introduction and documents provide students with a visual understanding of the meticulous and painstaking work that took place during the Scientific Revolution and the great imagination required in order for science to advance. The chronology provides a road map of the enormous change the many fields of science and medicine underwent over the course of several centuries. The questions for consideration ask students to draw broad comparisons and think critically about how and why each historical figure in this book contributed to the advance of science and medicine. Finally, the selected bibliography contains a wealth of sources for further student research.

A NOTE ABOUT THE TEXT

Spelling, punctuation, and capitalization in the documents have been modernized for ease of comprehension. In some cases, where a word was part of an original document's title (for example, Newton's *Thirty-first Query to the* OPTICKS, Document 12), the older spelling has been retained.

ACKNOWLEDGMENTS

Many hands helped make the material in this book accessible. Reviewers added their expertise to the shaping and revision of this book. They include Constantina Gaddis, Onondaga Community College;

Robert Hatch, University of Florida; Clayton Lehmann, University of South Dakota; Morag Martin, State University of New York–Brockport; Brian Ogilvie, University of Massachusetts Amherst; and Jana Pisani, Ferris State University. At Bedford/St. Martin's, Mary Dougherty, Jane Knetzger, Heidi Hood, Kathryn Abbott, Laurel Damashek, Katherine Flynn, Jennifer Jovin, Emily Berleth, Nancy Benjamin, and Kathleen Benn McQueen provided just the right level of guidance and advice.

   Not least, my own graduate students willingly read, corrected, and encouraged. The book is dedicated to them.

Margaret C. Jacob

Contents

Illustrations

THE BEDFORD SERIES IN HISTORY AND CULTURE

The Scientific Revolution

A Brief History with Documents

PART ONE

Introduction: The Evolution and Impact of the Scientific Revolution

In 1600, most Europeans stood on the earth, looked into the heavens, and confidently assumed that they were standing at the center of the universe. In that year, only a handful of people accepted Copernicus's argument, first made in 1543, that the sun, and not the earth, occupied the central place in our cosmos. As a learned Spanish Jesuit put the matter in 1590, "It is truly a wonderful thing to see how elegantly and gracefully Holy Writ" explains "that the earth and sea form a globe in the midst of the universe." By 1700, many educated people, especially in northern and western Europe, knew that Copernicus had been right and also knew that Isaac Newton's law of universal gravitation governed the motion of all the planets in relation to a stationary sun. By 1750, no European or American colonial could be considered educated if he or she still believed that the earth stood still and in the center of the universe, as the sun revolved around it. Even pocket almanacs or calendars aimed at the most general reader had begun to stop referring to a moving sun.[1]

The profound shift in the Western understanding of physical nature between the sixteenth and eighteenth centuries quickly acquired a shorthand description: the Scientific Revolution. Some have said that the phrase is misleading because it applies a political word—revolution—with all its implied suddenness, to a transformation that took well over a century and a half to unfold. But sometimes evolutionary change can

1

have a revolutionary impact. Scientific method is one of the distinctive features of modernity everywhere in the world, and, not surprisingly, those who hate the modern world are often hostile to science or favor occult or mystical forces that will provide an alternative set of explanations. Much more about nature than simply the physical mass placed in the center of the cosmos—the sun being substituted for the earth—altered as a result of the intellectual and cultural transformations brought about by the Scientific Revolution.

WHY DID THE SCIENTIFIC REVOLUTION HAPPEN?

The most challenging question is trying to determine why this transformation from ancient understandings of nature occurred in western Europe after 1500. This question is related to a larger one: Why did the West come to a position of global dominance by 1850? Much self-congratulation has accompanied many of the answers offered by Western historians over the years. But from any perspective, before 1700, China and much of Southeast Asia were technologically ahead of the West and just as intellectually vibrant. Chinese farmers could produce more food per acre and thus support the populations of far larger cities than those in the West. During the so-called Middle Ages of Europe, Arabic science and medicine were far in advance of Western science, and Arab scientists had extensive knowledge of ancient writers nearly forgotten in Europe. As one commentator notes, "Until 1750, changes in population, agriculture, technology, and living standards were not fundamentally different in eastern Asia from those in Western Europe." But by that date in the West, most universities in the northern areas of Europe and North America had stopped teaching Aristotle exclusively and had begun to teach the science and natural philosophy of Newton.[2]

Yet the land mass far to the west of China (what is called western Europe) had certain distinct characteristics that no one would have predicted to be advantageous. It was broken into rival and sovereign states, each possessing a different language. Although the Chinese emperor could control the ideas of his mandarin elite, no one in England could control what was being said—or published—in France. Even the Catholic Holy Roman Emperor could not stop people from becoming Protestants in his kingdom. The German-speaking areas of Europe in the sixteenth century were highly fragmented, with local princes and regions often going their separate ways and opting for the religion that they found most attractive. Relative to the power and hegemony of non-Western states, Western kings were weak. No common written language existed except Latin, and probably no more than 5 percent of the population could read it. Only the Christian church provided a universal point of reference to which rich and poor alike could respond.

After the Protestant Reformation began in 1517, the universalism of the Catholic Church was shattered, and Protestantism made deep inroads in many parts of Europe. More than a century of religious wars followed. If there was any single "cause" that made a few Europeans break with intellectual tradition and study nature differently, it was religious conflict. Catholics doubted the truth of Protestantism and vice versa, and doubt can be infectious. If something as venerable as the church could be questioned, even disdained, might not other truths bear scrutiny? Centers of non-clerical learning had emerged in the highly urbanized parts of Europe, on the Italian peninsula and in the Low Countries (including what is today parts of western Germany, the Netherlands, Belgium, and Luxembourg), as well as in London and Paris. Royal courts provided patronage and facilities where naturalists could work, presumably to enhance the glory of their princes. New forms of knowledge could flourish in places other than the universities, uniformly controlled as they were by the clergy, either Protestant or Catholic. Reformers intent on generating new knowledge about nature could gravitate to a court or a city. Access to the printing press was also vitally important. The competition to have naturalists, alchemists, and even astrologers at one's court made it impossible to keep their knowledge or experiments secret, leading to a science that was accessible to all who could read.

Historians still debate the causes of the Scientific Revolution. Some have argued that evidence from nature accumulated to the point that a major intellectual shift had to occur to accommodate it. Thus, these historians suggest that religious and social factors had little or nothing to do with the transformation away from Aristotle toward what came to be called the mechanical philosophy. Others have written books about the Scientific Revolution focused on a few great minds, claiming that the "revolution" never actually occurred. Still others have focused on the enduring role of the seemingly magical alchemy and questioned whether the so-called modern thinkers who ushered in the new science were really all that forward thinking.

The documents in this book provide evidence that a slow but real change occurred in the western European understanding of nature between 1550 and 1750 and that this shift had major implications for the development of the sciences, including medicine, as well as for advances in applied technology in everything from warfare to industry. The transformation toward a mechanical understanding of nature—the assumption that motion only occurs when bodies come into contact—was aided not only by new and better methods of observation but also by the expanded worldview of many Europeans as a result of overseas trade and exploration in the early modern era. Although theology dominated intellectual life in the sixteenth century, the seventeenth witnessed the emergence of more secular concerns, in part as a reaction to the turmoil unleashed by religious strife, by warfare between Catholics and Protestants. The continuous wars fought in the early modern period throughout Europe and against the Turks made the search for improved military technology a high priority. Competition, patronage, the printing press, the vitality of urban markets, and overseas trade and exploration all contributed to the rise of a new science. By 1800, universities were being founded—in Berlin, for example—that gave pride of place to "the scientific."

ARISTOTLE, PTOLEMY, AND THEIR EARLY MODERN DEFENDERS

When trying to understand the physical world, any educated person in early sixteenth-century Europe turned to the ancient philosopher Aristotle (384–322 BCE), as interpreted by generations of Christian scholars who controlled the great universities of Europe—Bologna in Italy, the Sorbonne in Paris, and Oxford and Cambridge in England. They proclaimed that only the principles of Aristotle, found in his *Physics* and interpreted by textbooks written by his followers, could explain why and how things moved, changed, or disintegrated. And Aristotle had said that the cause of change lies "in the nature of a thing."

Aristotle, as digested later by his many Christian followers and Arabic interpreters, stood as the most powerful influence in science until the seventeenth century. Certain aspects of Aristotelianism (often called *Scholasticism* because of its role in the curriculum of the schools) need emphasis. Aristotle saw the cosmos as a closed set of concentric spheres. At its center lay the earth. He believed the objects in the heavens were fixed and eternal, in effect perfect. If they moved, it was in perfectly circular orbits. The earth and things on or near its surface could degenerate or die, and the natural motions of earthly bodies that moved were rectilinear and perpendicular to the surface of the earth.

All natural substances were composed of matter and form. The stuff of which things were made—matter—had only the potential to be something. Only form could make matter into substance, imparting shape and the power to move. Form also determined the process or goal of a substance. Thus, rocks were endowed with heaviness by their form and naturally moved downward toward the earth, fire naturally rose, and plants and animals sought to reproduce and protect themselves. Humans were composed of form and matter, or soul and body, and they possessed an inherent goal of rationality. Immaterial forms shaped every physical thing, inanimate or living.

In the second century CE, the Alexandrian astronomer and mathematician Ptolemy (d. ca. 178 CE) fully articulated Aristotle's geocentric theory in the *Almagest*. Ptolemy wrote with what seemed to be common sense when he said that if the earth moved, people would be left riding in the air. Ptolemy appeared to explain what people on earth saw. Aristotle's ideas endured in part because they also proved flexible.

Christian philosophers easily adapted Aristotle to their ends; form became the immortal soul and its purpose lay in using reason to arrive at salvation. At the time of the Scientific Revolution, the most intellectually rigorous defense available of the Aristotelian position came from theologian and philosopher Francisco de Suarez (1548–1617). All the natural philosophers (who would later be called *scientists*) of the seventeenth century knew his writings well. It is impossible to comprehend the massive shift in ideas that occurred during the Scientific Revolution without understanding how Christian philosophers like the Jesuit Suarez described nature.[3]

Suarez articulated the central tenet of the Scholastic philosophy, the doctrine of form, which gave life, purpose, and meaning to matter. Forms could shape physical things, and they also had an existence beyond the physical—in the spiritual, or metaphysical—realm. Suarez wrote:

> It is indeed customary to divide form into physical and metaphysical; the prior . . . exerts true and real formal causality, and it is, therefore, that which we must treat most extensively. It is said to be a "physical form," either because it chiefly constitutes the nature of a thing, or because it is investigated principally through the analysis of physical change and is considered primarily in physics. Nevertheless, it is not outside the consideration of metaphysics. This is so, first, because the notion of "form" is common and abstract; then,

because form constitutes the essence of a thing; and, finally, because it is one of the principal causes. . . . It should, therefore, be said that, besides matter, all natural or corporeal things consist of substantial form as their intrinsic principle and formal cause. This is the view of Aristotle in innumerable places.[4]

Because Scholastics like Suarez linked the central concept of Aristotelian form to the religious idea of the human soul, any attack on the notion of form as the key to understanding nature had immediate and dire religious implications. As a Catholic priest, Suarez wanted to see the church's doctrines fortified philosophically at a time when the Protestant Reformation was challenging the pope and bitterness infused the relationship between Catholics and Protestants. It is not a coincidence that the most systematic attacks on Aristotle originated in Protestant circles where defeating his understanding of nature appeared to repudiate Catholic learning. No Catholic doctrine and practice depended more on Aristotle's forms than the sacrament of the Eucharist. During the Mass, the priest had the power to transform bread and wine into the body and blood of Christ because the form of the matter could be changed without affecting its shape or appearance.

EXPLORATION AND TECHNOLOGICAL INNOVATION

The contestation and eventual displacement of Scholasticism did not occur in an intellectual vacuum, in minds divorced from everyday realities. It is not accidental that the attack on Aristotle coincided with the explosive growth of overseas trade and exploration. Suddenly, the Spanish, Portuguese, Dutch, English, and French were encountering people, plants, and animals never before imagined. With this opening of the European mind came much hardship and abuse for the peoples conquered or enslaved, or both. It also challenged the force of tradition and authority at home. Why had the ancient philosophers not foreseen the richness, complexity, and diversity that existed throughout the globe? Why is there no mention of the Americas in the Bible? By the mid-seventeenth century, Europeans' knowledge of distant people and places had grown exponentially. By 1700, more than 160 accounts had been published to describe the indigenous peoples of the Americas alone. Naturalists even vied for the chance to travel in the merchant ships bound for the New World, and the artist and naturalist Maria Sibylla Merian (1647–1717) went so far as to finance her own trip and that of her daughter to the Dutch colony of Suriname so that she could observe its plants, animals, bugs, and insects firsthand (see Document 14). So much movement of goods and people even suggested that a new mathematics was needed, one that could better express the movement of bodies.

In addition, travelers' encounters with Hindus, Muslims, and Jews— as well as the indigenous people of the New World—made it harder to assume that everything Western must by definition be right or universal. Francis Bacon (1561–1626), one of the intellectual lights of the Scientific Revolution, articulated the link between the new science and overseas exploration; it is God's will, he said, that "the circumnavigation of the world and the increase of the sciences should happen in the same age" (see Document 2).[5]

The global expansion of Europe occurred at a time of deep intellectual and religious ferment. The printing press, a German invention of the mid-fifteenth century, allowed for unprecedented access to books in every language and in every country. Protestants and Catholics debated their respective religious differences through print. In all countries, some form of censorship, often imposed by the clergy, sought to control what could be printed. Natural philosophers seized on the press for communicating their disagreement with Aristotle or their new theories and mathematical evidence about the way nature operated. Invented around the same time, copperplate engraving proved invaluable in scientific books intended to illustrate in detail what the naturalist had seen or discovered.

Many practitioners of the new science broke with tradition even in the language they used to communicate their findings. Instead of using Latin, the language of philosophy, they turned to their native languages and sought to reach an educated audience that might only read in Italian or French or English. Increasingly, the new natural philosophers published books containing pictures that reinforced abstract ideas or depicted new devices and machines, as well as showing the interior of the human body or the structure of insects.

Crafts such as lens grinding, engraving, and metal working were the domain of artisans, not intellectuals. Often overlooked in the study of the Scientific Revolution has been the artisanal contribution to its momentum, as hundreds of working men and women put into practice what would come to be seen as a new empirical science. In London alone by 1600, there were at least two thousand practitioners of science, women herbalists, male and female alchemists (alchemy was the pharmacology of the day), botanists, distillers, printers, machinists, and clock makers. All contributed innovative practices that added precision, rigor, and newly accumulated information, and they laid a foundation for what would eventually be called the Scientific Revolution.[6]

In addition, technological innovations helped spur the massive innovations in the Western understanding of nature. The new telescopes and microscopes of the age made possible investigations never before imagined. The improvement in lens grinding enabled these endeavors and also produced better and cheaper eyeglasses that expanded people's working lives and reading capabilities. Sometimes new technology permitted new science; other times, the relationship was reversed. For example, Galileo Galilei's (1564–1642) ability to "see" the earth's moon and the moons of Jupiter (see Document 4) was critically important to his success, but he had to know how to interpret what the improved telescope allowed him to see. He put his eye to the glass with a set of philosophical assumptions, and one was the uniformity of matter. Once he saw the shadows on the moon, he could postulate that the moon was a physical body.

Sometimes the science led to technological innovations. By 1700, the science of mechanics had been systematized with books and lectures explaining how better to distribute weight; how to use levers, pulleys, and balances to greater effect in everything from making better carriages to lifting water out of coal mines. Mechanical knowledge

Figure 1. *A Steam-Powered Carriage, 1789.*
The engineer who made this carriage was thinking ahead of the times but only by a few years. The obvious next step with the steam engine lay in its application to transportation.
Courtesy of the Society of Antiquaries of Newcastle upon Tyne.

spread, and its penetration became particularly evident in eighteenth-century Britain. It is easily understood why the first steam engines came out of circles familiar with Robert Boyle's concept of the "weight of the air," what we call *air pressure*. The engine's rapid spread was the work of engineers familiar with Newtonian mechanics. By the late eighteenth century, its power had been applied to mining and manufacturing, and inventors were trying to figure out how it might be applied to transportation. It became what economists call a general-purpose technology (like computers today) and, by 1800, it would be adapted to a wide variety of tasks requiring power. By the mid-nineteenth century, the British possessed engines that delivered ten times the power of any that could be found in France. Innovation translated into national power and empire.

THE EMERGENCE OF THE SCIENTIFIC REVOLUTION

By the time of the Industrial Revolution (1780–1850), the vision of the Aristotelians had long since been dismantled. But dismantling that vision would take more than a century and require a series of philosophical challenges. Aristotle's natural philosophy gave an inherent purpose and motion to earthly objects and a distinctive and ethereal nature to heavenly ones. Its defeat required the recovery and adaptation of other ancient philosophies. The Italian Renaissance of the fifteenth and early sixteenth centuries had brought back into circulation long-forgotten philosophies by ancient philosophers such as Plato (ca. 428–348 BCE) and Epicurus (341–270 BCE). Plato emphasized the invisible forces at work in nature and argued that appearances could be deceiving. Mathematics held the key to nature and revealed its inherent harmony. The Epicureans are today largely remembered for wanting to have a good time, but that is a distortion of a basic philosophy that emphasized personal virtue. Europeans of the early modern period knew the thought of Epicurus largely through the poem by his follower Lucretius (ca. 99–55 BCE), *De rerum natura*. Its importance lay in the atomism it preached—that nature was composed of miniscule, hard corpuscles that randomly combine to create the bodies that can be seen by our eyes. It also proposed that there were multiple worlds, that our universe was not alone in the cosmos. Epicureans denied that all the bodies in nature possessed a goal, thus breaking with Aristotle's ideas about form and purpose.

Along with ancient atomism and the Platonic emphasis on mathematical elegance came the revival of the ancient philosophies of skepticism and Stoicism. As the religious wars of the sixteenth century intensified, both on the battlefields and in print, each of these philosophies seemed viable alternatives to competing religious dogmas and doctrines preached from whatever pulpit. The skeptics rejected the dogmatism found in both the Protestant and Catholic churches and argued that ultimate truth was not available to human beings. The Stoics urged that reason control the passions, especially in religious matters, and that detachment is the only ethically viable posture. Both skepticism and Stoicism played a role in offering alternatives to Aristotle and in lending support to aspects of the new science—its willingness to doubt received wisdom and its emphasis on slow, painstaking labor.

Seldom has a doctrine aroused greater animosity than the doctrine of forms, and, gradually and firmly, the new science discarded it. In its place came new practices and philosophical assumptions, what is generally called the *mechanical philosophy*. This philosophy assumed that all motion occurs as the result of contact between bodies. There are no inherent tendencies to either rest or move. Mathematics can best describe these motions, and it began to replace metaphysics as the tool for unlocking nature's secrets. As the metaphysical assumption of form was discarded, new atomic explanations for matter and motion replaced it. Matter was composed of small, hard, impenetrable bodies. Some called them *corpuscles* and said that they could be divided infinitely. Others called them *atoms*, the smallest, hard and impenetrable material of which things in nature are composed. The motion of bodies became possible not because form "told" them how to move; rather, they moved if they were hit by another body. If they were not hit, they remained inert. The Western thinkers who rejected Scholasticism and established the theories, proofs, and practices that became known as the Scientific Revolution redefined physical matter, motion, space and time, the nature of light, the substance and orbits of the heavenly bodies, the value of mathematics and its ability to describe moving bodies, and, not least, the motions of the human body from the circulation of blood to the structure of the lymphatic system.

THE NEW SCIENCE

Many historians of the Scientific Revolution date its beginning to Nicolaus Copernicus (1473–1543). Raised by a pious uncle who eventually became a bishop, Copernicus also held a church office; his intellectual interests, however, were in studying physical nature, the heavens, and the human body. As a young student at Cracow University in what is today Poland, Copernicus studied Aristotelian philosophy. After studying at Bologna where he probably encountered the writings of Plato, Copernicus began lecturing in mathematics and studying astronomy. In addition, he was a doctor of canon law and a physician. In 1540, one of his pupils, Rheticus, began to circulate the idea that the earth moved around the sun, not vice versa. Copernicus agreed to publish the theory he had been teaching in *De Revolutionibus orbium coelestium* (see Document 1). Legend has it that Copernicus received the final proof sheets of the book when on his deathbed in May 1543, months before the book was published. In articulating a heliocentric theory of the universe, Copernicus broke with Aristotle and his ancient follower Ptolemy.[7] By no means, however, was Copernicus immediately accepted. Decades later, Suarez wrote as if Copernicus was irrelevant. As all Copernicus's contemporaries knew, it is not self-evident that the earth moves. But Copernicus believed that by simplifying the mathematics needed to explain the motions of the planets, he had edged closer to philosophical truth.

Copernicus was also a medical doctor, and he would have known about new developments in medicine. By the mid-sixteenth century, medical reform was very much a burning issue. A contemporary of Copernicus, Andreas Vesalius (1514–1564), produced a massive work in seven volumes, *On the Structure of the Human Body* (1543), that gave the world the most detailed study ever done on every aspect of the human body. Its use of engraving to illustrate every organ, muscle, and fiber was unprecedented and provided a kind of "map" that other anatomists and physicians used for decades.

Observation was also a critical part of the new aesthetic at the root of innovative science. Tycho Brahe (1546–1601) took planetary observation to new standards of accuracy and even discovered new stars. He did all of this without accepting Copernican heliocentrism, thus illustrating that observation could flourish independently from the bold theoretical claims that would come to define the new science. Perhaps his greatest contribution to the new science came from his decision to hire the young German Johannes Kepler (1571–1630). Possibly out of jealousy at Kepler's brilliance, Brahe set him up with the nearly impossible task of plotting the orbit of Mars by using Brahe's observations. Gradually, almost painfully, Kepler came to see that Aristotle must have been wrong when he decreed that all motion in the heavens had to be perfectly circular. Only a flattened circle, an ellipse,

Kepler realized, could account for all the places that Mars ventures as it circumnavigates the sun. With that insight, he went on to formulate three laws of planetary motion that proved to be critical for the work done by seventeenth-century natural philosophers.

Note that so far we have been describing the contributions made by a Pole (Copernicus), a Belgian (Vesalius), a Dane (Brahe), an Italian (Galileo), and a German (Kepler). An international conversation that transcended national and linguistic borders as well as religious convictions characterized the early decades of the new scientific inquiry. That would change gradually over the course of the seventeenth century as science became increasingly a northern European phenomenon with a strongly Protestant demography. Intellectual preeminence in science became associated with the English, Dutch, and French.

Inspired by the Protestant Reformation, Francis Bacon began the intellectual assault on scholastic practices. Bacon often gets credit for singlehandedly advancing the cause of English science when in fact he was riding on the crest of a wave of scientific practitioners at work in London during the reign of Elizabeth I (r. 1558–1603) and beyond. Bacon's education at Cambridge University left him with a lifelong dislike of Aristotle and his interpreters, while his career as a lawyer encouraged his bent toward research and empirical evidence. He believed that what the age called "politiques" (politics) should be the calling of a few gifted and experienced men, eager to serve their princes. Bacon spent his life essentially in two pursuits: advancement at court, first under Elizabeth I and then more spectacularly under King James I (r. 1603–1625). Just as earnestly, Bacon worked to lay the foundations for new attitudes toward learning, in particular the study of the natural world. The second of these activities made him famous among the educated and eventually inspired the new adjective "Baconian." It described the detailed examination of nature, a collecting and sifting, an interrogation of it with an eye toward useful application. Bacon also advocated that the king and the state take up the cause of science (see Document 2).

Bacon urged his readers to get out into nature—to explore, to test, to experience—in the search for human improvement, possibly even perfectibility (see Document 3). Bacon wanted learning to become a way to God similar to what the Bible offered. God's work would complement his word. As a servant of the prince and his state, Bacon also realized that science could enhance the power of the state. He was the first to see what many European and eventually American governments came to believe—that science in the service of the state increases its power. Baconianism came to be associated with the dedication to science and utility found in philosophical circles throughout northern Europe. When the French revolutionaries of the 1790s opened the first ever exposition of industrial technology and fine craftsmanship, they invoked Bacon as their inspiration.[8]

THE MECHANICAL PHILOSOPHY

Beginning in the late 1580s, Galileo Galilei began the process by which the central tenets of the mechanical philosophy were put into place. Born in Pisa, Galileo started life within a learned, artisanal household. His father possessed musical and mathematical skills, and Galileo received an education first from a private tutor and then at the university in Pisa. His background gave him enormous self-confidence. Increasingly, Galileo's interests drew him to mathematics and physics. Around 1583, he discovered that when taking small swings, a pendulum always swings to and fro in the same period of time regardless of the length of the swing.

Circumstances drew Galileo to Florence where his research into natural phenomena expanded in new and exciting directions. He earned the respect and patronage of the Florentine court and was connected with high society in both church and state.

Early in his career, Galileo came to oppose Aristotle's influence on the physical sciences. Galileo was able to demonstrate that bodies of unequal weight fall at the same speed, a principle that contradicted the Scholastic notion that the weight of a body determined its trajectory. Galileo's discoveries laid the foundation for a mechanical understanding of nature and the idea that bodies remain at rest until hit by another body and not because of a condition "natural" to them. Central to the mechanical understanding of nature lay the notion that all of nature is composed of matter in motion. In *The Starry Messenger*, published in 1610 (Document 4), Galileo argued that the matter in the heavens is the same as that on earth. His work depended on Copernican theory, skepticism toward the Scholastics, and a good measure of observation. Galileo was convinced that Copernicus was right. Because the moon revolved around the earth, the moon's being a body added weight to the Copernican hypothesis; why could not the earth, another body, revolve around the sun? Having seen the contours of the earth's moon, the four moons of Jupiter, and new planets through his superior telescope, Galileo proclaimed that the earth and the heavens are made of the same material substance.

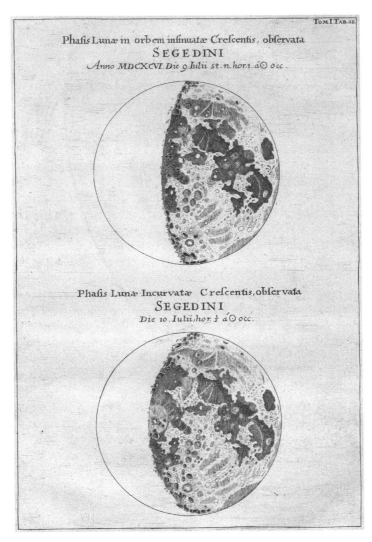

Figure 2. *Galileo Galilei, Two Illustrations of the Moon, 1610.*
Galileo's knowledge of artistic technique—that is, the use of lighter and darker shades to denote distance and contours—may have been critical to the way he saw the moon. Once his eye spotted the shadows on it, he concluded that what he observed could only be physical shapes. The moon became a physical body, not a ball of ethereal light and, like the earth it possessed mountains and valleys (see Document 4).

Department of Special Collections, Charles E. Young Research Library, UCLA.

14

As a devout Catholic, Galileo knew that his heliocentric assumption would not sit well with the Roman Catholic Church. Indeed in 1616, the church had condemned the Copernican argument because it said that the argument contradicted passages in the Bible. In the early 1630s, Galileo took up his pen and defended Copernicus even though the church had expressly forbidden such defense. Because the Bible suggested that the earth stood still and because the church reserved the right to interpret matters of truth—even in natural philosophy— the church put Galileo on trial for heresy. The church may also have believed that Galileo's embrace of a form of atomism introduced a theory of matter that would ultimately undermine the doctrine of transubstantiation, the belief that the priest has the power to change the form of bread and wine, turning it into the body and blood of Christ.

In 1633, the Catholic Inquisition in Rome declared "that you, the said Galileo, by reason of the matters adduced in trial...have rendered yourself...vehemently suspected of heresy, namely, of having believed...that the sun is the center of the world and does not move from east to west and that the earth moves and is not center of the world."[9] Galileo was fortunate in only being condemned to house arrest and not prison—or worse. At an official ceremony in 1992, Pope John Paul II admitted that the church had made a grave error. But in Galileo's lifetime and long after, his overconfident challenge to papal authority was ignored, and for supporters of the new science he became one of its "martyrs."[10]

At the same time that Galileo and others were making enormous advances in physics, mathematics, and astronomy, other scientists turned to experiments on animals to try to better understand the functioning of corporeal bodies. William Harvey (1578–1657), trained in medicine and anatomy at Padua, was educated in the doctrines of the Greek physician Galen (ca. 130–201) who largely followed Aristotle. Thus Harvey believed himself to be working in the tradition of Aristotelian medicine when he did his anatomical work, using, as was the custom, live dogs so that the flow of blood could be observed as it was happening. He was not so much experimental as observational when he argued that logic dictates that blood circulates (see Document 5). Harvey taught anatomy and surgery at London's Royal College of Physicians. Being both innovative and Aristotelian was still possible in Harvey's lifetime, although his would be the last generation in England in which that combination remained credible.

The Catholic Church's opposition to Copernicanism had very real effects on the life of perhaps the most important mechanical thinker of the Scientific Revolution, René Descartes (1596–1650). No one natural philosopher in the period from 1600 to 1700 did more to put the mechanical philosophy in place than Descartes. Educated by Jesuits at one of the best schools in France, Descartes was among the pupils who read about Galileo's great discoveries in *The Starry Messenger.* Descartes grew up in an age of religious wars between Catholics and Protestants. In reaction, some philosophers turned to skepticism as the only civilized response to such bloodshed; why not doubt everything when true believing leads to death, destruction, and the collapse of social order? As an antidote, Descartes sought to create a method for arriving at clear and distinct ideas guided only by reason and to illustrate it by three experiments with natural objects. Following Galileo's condemnation in 1633, Descartes removed himself to the Protestant Dutch Republic. He was deeply influenced by Galileo, knew the arguments of Bacon, and believed that a mechanical understanding of nature—that it is made of minuscule corpuscles and that contact between bodies accounts for motion—was the only foundation on which to build a new science. These principles applied not only to earthly motion but also to the motion of the planets. Descartes embraced the mechanical philosophy as part of a life-altering, moral enterprise that required an entirely new intellectual posture in the world. Descartes explained that nature had mathematical laws and that the matter of the universe was not only uniform but also put—and kept—in motion because of these laws. And Descartes made the study of these mathematical laws into an ethical enterprise, a search for truth that was public, open, modest (at least rhetorically), and (theoretically) available to anyone who would reason and seek to understand nature clearly and distinctly. To do that, however, such a person had to be anchored in his or her own mind; the work of natural philosophy required self-awareness—or, as Descartes put it, "I think therefore I am."

How to become the new kind of person who embraced his own clear and distinct ideas was the subject of Descartes' famous *Discourse on Method* (1637) (see Document 6). The tone taken throughout suggests humility and a willingness to address literate artisans, not just other masters of philosophy. Descartes was also deeply interested in anatomy and health in general, all subjects he pursued in conversation with Dutch doctors and colleagues. In turn, Dutch universities were among the first to teach his science, although not without enormous resistance from numerous faculty, both Protestant and Catholic, who remained Scholastics.[11]

Living as a Cartesian, inspired by Descartes' writings, could take many forms. Descartes' most innovative arguments centered on the human passions. Rather than moralize about and repress emotions, Descartes treated them as involuntary actions that simply are. Writers inspired by his vision turned to literature as the vehicle that could move the passions of the soul; art theorists urged a turn away from formalism toward a freer use of the brush, an attempt to evoke emotion and move the passions. Medical practitioners tried to understand the body, particularly pain, as the involuntary movement of atoms that put pressure on the tissues of the brain. All sought to better understand the mechanisms that united feeling with the senses, the mind with the body. Before Descartes, various schools of philosophy had urged the repression of emotion and the disciplining of sensual experience.

Cartesian understandings of nature were often taken up by thinkers far less pious than Descartes who could use Cartesian thinking to justify materialism—the belief that the world is nothing more than matter in motion, divorced from spirits and souls, even from divinity. Most of the leaders of the Scientific Revolution were devout Christians, but others, generally their readers or followers, sometimes used the new scientific ideas to embrace what the age called "deism" or "freethinking." Some in fact became atheists. By 1700, a coherent explanation of how the universe worked could be articulated without reference to God.

If nature is seen as Descartes saw it, composed of minuscule corpuscles, small and (for the most part) flexible particles, then surely these could be removed, leaving only vacant space. That is precisely what Robert Boyle (1627–1691) did with his air pump (see Document 7). No one would have predicted that this young aristocrat, the youngest son of the immensely wealthy Earl of Cork, born a Protestant in Ireland and destined for a life of leisure, travel, and the hunt, would turn himself into the model of the scientific work ethic and inspire an entire generation. But in the 1640s, Boyle experienced a religious conversion that brought him close to Puritanism, and he became an exceptionally devout Protestant. This happened at the moment when the English Parliament, led by the Puritans, had turned against King Charles I and the Anglican Church, and civil war raged in England, Ireland, and Scotland. Boyle also became a practicing alchemist, and reading alchemical texts turned him in the direction of atomism.[12]

Boyle's circle favored Parliament and the Puritan cause and, like so many on that side of the revolution then sweeping the country, Boyle believed that he lived in an unprecedented age of reformation. Learning would be transformed and the changes would bring about a new

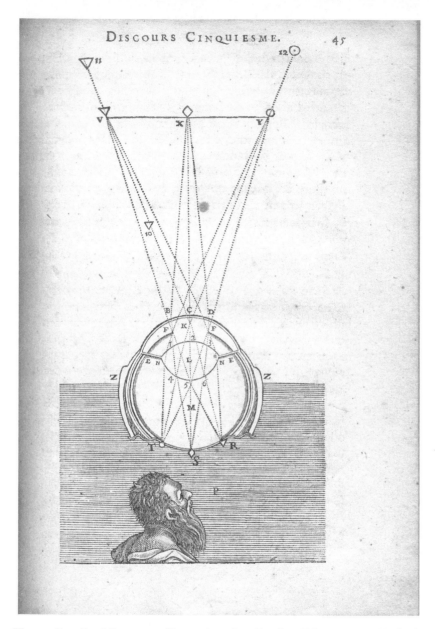

Figure 3. *René Descartes, Illustration of an Eye from* Discourse on Method, *1637.*

Here Descartes tries to illustrate the impact of light corpuscles on the eye, always traceable with mathematical precision.

Department of Special Collections, Charles E. Young Research Library, UCLA.

18

republic of learning and possibly foreshadow the arrival of a millennial paradise on earth. Christ would literally come again and institute a thousand-year reign of peace and prosperity. First Boyle laid out for himself an entire ethical system that turned away from privilege and birth, emphasizing good works and virtue. He then turned to alchemy and chemistry, and experimentation more generally. He used microscopes and, most importantly, sought a new philosophical anchor for his investigations. Boyle was guided in his early work by the alchemist and atomist, Daniel Sennert (1572–1637).

Deeply moved by Descartes and Sennert, Boyle united mechanical philosophy's assumptions with experimental protocol, essentially perfecting modern experimental techniques by insisting on replication and by describing his experiments in such minute detail that the results could be tested. In addition, as one of the founders of London's Royal Society, Boyle was a key player in the social organization of the new science. He saw himself as both a Baconian and a Cartesian, and he labored all his life to defeat Scholasticism. Unlike Descartes, Boyle sought not to make bold generalizations but to carefully amass information, replicate it, and offer it to the world as a tentative conclusion. He also took a posture of caution and invented a scientific style that was skeptical and attentive to detail. But when it came to what he called "philosophical theories," he firmly concluded, "If but a full light of experiments and observations be freely let in upon them, the beauty of those (delightful, but phantastical) structures does immediately vanish." The doctrine of form was one such theory.[13]

With Boyle's contributions to the experimental method, the characteristic features of modern science came clearly into focus. Nature consisted of material atoms; matter is weight and when subjected to pressure of another body, it moves. Boyle's ability to create a vacuum in a sealed glass jar, a device specially made for the purpose, proved the existence of air pressure or, as Boyle put it, the weight of the air. Men associated with Boyle's laboratory went on to invent some of the first steam engines that harnessed that weight by creating a vacuum in a cylinder. When filled with steam, it raised a beam, and, when turned into a vacuum by cold water evaporating the steam, it allowed the beam to fall. Mechanics, or what we generally call "mechanical engineering," was then put in place gradually, beginning late in the seventeenth century.

Boyle said that he had undertaken scientific work not only for the glory of God but also to show that modern learning had become superior to that of the ancients. To say that nature abhors a vacuum, as did

Aristotle, has the effect of endorsing what Boyle called "the vulgarly received notion of nature" (see Document 8). Boyle sought to defeat Aristotle as part of a larger project of removing the intellectual underpinnings of Catholic doctrine. He, like Bacon before him, believed that studying nature was a Protestant act of piety in the service of God. This vision of the purpose of science eventually became commonplace throughout Europe. In 1785 when the first scientific society for women opened its doors in the Dutch Republic, the lecturer of the day invoked these pious sentiments, what came to be called "physico-theology."

The mechanical philosophy was by no means the exclusive province of the wealthy and educated. Anthony van Leeuwenhoek (1632–1723) was the son of a basket maker who never attended a university. He represents one of the most remarkable aspects of the movement toward a new science—an artisan who became the discoverer of new worlds. Leeuwenhoek made his own microscopes. These microscopes were generally only about three inches long, and some may have magnified at five hundred times the size of the object. Only about nine have survived and one of those can magnify at two hundred seventy-five times. No one had an instrument as fine, and it was well over one hundred fifty years before microscopes would become more powerful.

With his powerful microscopes, Leeuwenhoek saw many things in nature for the first time. He observed the bacteria on his own teeth (see Document 9), the wings of flies, and the algae in ponds. He was methodical and endlessly patient, and he recorded his experiments in such a way that they could be replicated. When he could not read a work because it was not available in Dutch, he sought out translators. In short, he was a cosmopolitan, conversant with the latest microscopic work being done in Europe, and he was not afraid to disagree with other experimenters when he thought they had made an error. A small inheritance and a municipal position in his native town of Delft gave Leeuwenhoek the time to devote himself almost entirely to microscopic investigations. For his many achievements, he was made a Fellow of the Royal Society of London.

Leeuwenhoek's work bears a remarkable resemblance to that of his contemporary, the German-born artist and naturalist, Maria Sibylla Merian. Although Merian was a trained artist and Leeuwenhoek came from more humble origins, both were essentially artisans. They belonged to the class of investigators that historians have come to understand as absolutely fundamental to the social foundations of the

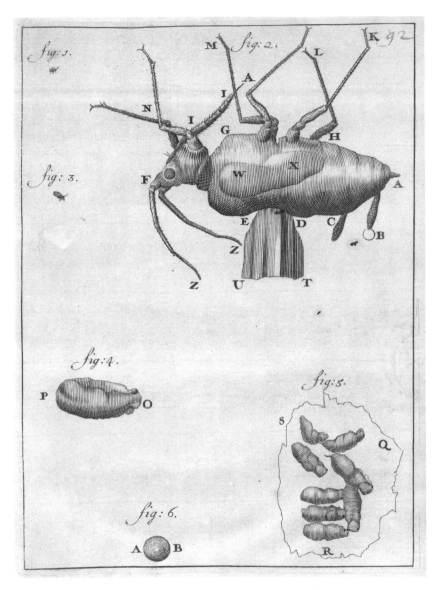

Figure 4.   *Anthony van Leeuwenhoek, Illustration of a Flea, 1696.*
This engraving by van Leeuwenhoek illustrates the importance of pictures in conveying new natural philosophical knowledge.
Department of Special Collections, Charles E. Young Research Library, UCLA.

21

new science. Inspired by religion, Merian sought to know God's creation at a level of detail previously unimagined. Her artistic skills combined with immense personal courage and, with her daughter in tow, she sailed to see the jungles of South America to record in meticulous detail the metamorphosis of the insects of Suriname (see Document 14). Merian began her study of nature by catching caterpillars in her garden at the age of thirteen. She made watercolors of their transformation into butterflies and, just as important, she kept meticulous journals where she recorded everything that she saw systematically. Her father had been an engraver and a printer in Germany who did superb illustrations for alchemical works that he published. Her first two illustrated books written in German dealt with caterpillars and their remarkable transformation into butterflies, beetles, or flies (see Document 15).

Relocated to Amsterdam, Merian saw the many exotic specimens brought back by the Dutch trading companies. The religious sect she had joined there, the mystical Labadists, had also established a community in Suriname, possibly in expectation of the second coming of Christ. With great peril, in 1699 Merian set out on a voyage of six to eight weeks to join the Labadists and to see tropical insects and animals in their native habitat. Using slaves or native servants who brought her specimens from the jungles or sugar plantations, Merian did not always correctly place her specimens in the right "family." She was nevertheless the first person to describe and depict the pineapple in its own habitat, to present in detail the life cycle of the cockroach, and to offer extensive commentary on cotton, potatoes, yams and tomatoes, crocodiles, snakes, and lizards. She even brought a native woman back with her to Amsterdam as she was dependent on her knowledge of the indigenous flora and fauna. In so doing, Merian revolutionized the study of zoology. Both Leeuwenhoek and Merian alert us to the enormous contributions made by ordinary people to the new empirically based science.

NEWTONIAN SCIENCE

Bacon, Galileo, Kepler, Descartes, and Boyle all set the stage for the appearance of Newtonian science. Arguably the greatest mathematical and philosophical thinker of the Scientific Revolution, Isaac Newton (1642–1727) was born to neither luxury nor high learning. As a student at Cambridge University, he waited on tables. Forced to flee the town because of the appearance of bubonic plague in 1665, Newton found the time and solitude to develop his mathematical skills, to apply the new science of mechanics to the earth's motion, to investigate the nature of light, and to position himself—unknown at the time to anyone else—as the greatest living natural philosopher in the Western world. Cambridge gave him a professorship and there he remained until the early 1690s, when he went to London to become Master of the Mint.

Newton followed scores of original thinkers—as he put it, "I stand on the shoulders of giants." Boyle's vacuum was critically important for enabling Newton to break with Descartes' insistence that the heavens were filled with a fine material substance that swirled in vortices (as Descartes named them). Mechanically, the pressure they exerted on the planets held them in place. Newton accepted the mechanical vision of Galileo and Descartes and then radically transformed it when he applied it to the heavens. The mechanical philosophy insisted that all motions be caused by the impact of other bodies in motion, and hence denied that any invisible forces could act across a distance without the mediation of other bodies in motion, however ethereal they were. Newton, by contrast, demonstrated that all bodies evince an attraction to one another—a universal gravitation that he postulated took place across empty spaces. Newton presumed that universal gravitation worked in the vacuum of absolute space, in what he called "the sensorium" of God.

Newton's notebooks from his days at Cambridge University reveal not only his religious piety but also his intense study of the natural philosophers of the age. We tend to think of Newton as a great physicist—possibly the greatest before Albert Einstein. This is true, but it should not let us forget that he was also arguably one of the most powerful philosophical minds of the seventeenth century. Philosophical convictions, in particular a deep commitment to an atomic hypothesis, enabled Newton to embark on his optical experiments. He believed light to be composed of atomic particles (not waves) and thus he thought that it might be possible to disaggregate it. The prism experiments proved light to be a composite, that "light consists of rays differently refrangible." Each color would pass through a set of prisms at a different angle. Again, new experimental techniques put in place an orthodoxy that seemed to run against all observations. Sunlight had been regarded always as simple, homogeneous, and pure with colors being imagined as some sort of modification of sunlight. Newton argued that colors are "original and connate properties" of light. Colors appear when they are separated from sunlight; they are never created.

Indeed Newton's earliest publication, a paper sent to the Royal Society, was on color (see Document 10). In this paper on color, Newton never presented atomism. That theory served only as a hypothesis for Newton and as such remained unaddressed in his scientific writings. As he said repeatedly, "I do not feign hypotheses."

Not only did Newton embrace atomism, but he also acquired a belief in the power of invisible but knowable forces in nature. In the preface to the *Principia* (see Document 11), he called these forces "attractive or impulsive." These, he believed, had been known by the ancient philosophers, a wisdom that now could be recaptured because recent philosophers had "dismissed substantial forms and occult qualities." In the *Principia*, Newton put in place a rational as well as a practical mechanics. In the *Principia*, he grounded mechanics as well as celestial dynamics in geometry. In his subsequent works, however, Newton took mathematics a step further with the development of calculus. Newton's laws of force made possible a calculation as to the amount of work done by a certain volume of water falling from a known height, or the amount of work it would take to raise a certain weight a known distance. Thus, calculus provided a quicker and more flexible mathematics than geometry for describing bodies in motion.

Amid all the propositions and geometrical reasoning lies the centerpiece of the *Principia*: the establishment of universal gravitation and its use to demonstrate the elliptical orbits of the planets. In the first thirteen propositions of Book III, Newton derives the law of universal gravitation—that the planet is kept in its elliptical orbit because all bodies attract one another, a force that is inversely proportional to their distance from one another (according to their masses). The elliptical orbit results from the centripetal force pulling the planet toward the sun (or another planet). When accused of introducing an "occult force" into natural philosophy—because the action of gravity was through space at a distance—the second edition of the *Principia* shot back with the simple statement, "Gravity can by no means be called an occult cause . . . because it is plain from the phenomena that such a power does really exist." Newton further proclaimed that "the business of true philosophy is to derive the nature of things from causes truly existent." In answer to the question "What is gravity?" Newton said only that he had solely to prove mathematically that gravity operated throughout the universe, not to define it. Newton's method of reasoning about nature, going from an analysis by experimentation to a synthesis or general principle, to be tested again by analysis, became the methodological foundation of all scientific work.

Figure 5. *Giovanni Battista Piton, "An Allegorical Monument to Sir Isaac Newton," 1741.*

Painted by Piton in 1741, the image is an apotheosis of Newton's great achievement in demonstrating the multiple rays that constitute "white light."

The Fitzwilliam Museum.

25

Newton's universe was alive with invisible forces or, as he put it in one manuscript never published, "All nature is attended with signs of life." Such natural forces could make for chemical transformations and effect radical change. They were the source of earthquakes and tidal waves, and other dramatic changes visible in nature. These same forces worked on transforming ordinary substances. Newton was a practicing alchemist for most of his life, and he believed that some day someone truly adept would rearrange the atoms and succeed in transforming base metal into gold. Ironically, in the course of his alchemical work, best glimpsed through the *Thirty-first Query to the* OPTICKS (see Document 12), Newton put the science of chemistry on a firmer footing. He states his assumption in the form of a question at the opening of the thirty-first query, "Have not the small particles of bodies certain powers, virtues, or forces by which they act at a distance?" He believed that the new science would uncover those forces. When later in the eighteenth century European philosophers turned toward vitalism—a belief that life infused the material—they were developing hints found in the thirty-first query. For his achievements, Newton was awarded a knighthood and buried in Westminster Abbey. Artists also tried to demonstrate the majestic accomplishments of his optics. Poets sang, "Let Newton be, and all is light." Much of the adulation would have been lost on Newton, who paid little attention to either art or poetry. Something of a recluse, he never married and died in the home of his niece, leaving in the Bank of England the remarkable wealth of £14,000.[14]

RECONCILING SCIENCE, RELIGION, AND MAGIC

Bold and new ideas followed from the mechanical philosophy, but so too did new arguments for religion. Both Catholics and Protestants argued that the study of nature and the heavens reveals design, the hand of the deity as it instills order. Pious Protestants like Christiaan Huygens (1629–1695), Boyle, and Newton (who encountered English freethinkers in their own time) recoiled from the materialistic implications of the new science. They believed that science confirmed God's divine intervention into nature, not its ability to order itself. A science-supported Protestantism offered an alternative to both materialism and Catholicism, they insisted. As late as the 1780s, a Dutch scientific society for women justified its existence by arguing that the study of nature was an act of piety; members started with lessons in mechanics. A hundred years earlier, Boyle saw that to defeat Scholasticism once and for all and to prove the mechanical philosophy definitively, results had to be visible, tangible, and replicable. But how to achieve them?

Over time, dozens of early modern contributors, both Catholic and Protestant, brought down the edifice of Scholasticism. Naturalists, alchemists, herbalists, physicians, armchair philosophers, anatomists, botanists, and mathematicians all had a hand in chipping away at the certainty that Aristotle and his Scholastic philosophers once imparted. Both astrology and alchemy played an important role in the beliefs of many early modern natural philosophers. For example, both Brahe and Kepler devoted a great deal of their time as astronomers and natural philosophers trying to improve astrology rather than discard it. At the same time, Kepler was a devoted Copernican.

That Brahe, Kepler, Galileo, and many other innovators of the new science all had legitimate interests in astrology—and there was nothing in the Aristotelian tradition that told them that having the stars influence human behavior was a bad idea—tells us that they were active courtiers, eager to work for their respective princes. Whether in Prague or Florence, courts expected advice that would potentially save them from ruinous decisions, and they thought that astrology might just give it. Similarly in its early years, the Paris Academy of Science, under court patronage from Louis XIV, pursued alchemy with much diligence. It promised improved pharmacology but also, at its most ambitious, the discovery of elixirs of life and even the transformation of base metals into gold. Princes like ordinary mortals aspired to great wealth and longevity, and they had the money to pay people to pursue both. Natural philosophers, in turn, quite often needed patronage to survive, especially in a world where the clergy and Scholastics controlled the universities. The Paris academy was eventually told by the king's representative to stop "the great work" of alchemy and get on with the business of mapping France. But in that year, 1685, Louis XIV had grand imperial plans to purge France of all Protestants and to expand French territory into the Low Countries. Safe in England, Boyle and Newton continued their alchemical pursuits privately, and it was only after 1700 that alchemy and astrology were firmly classified, where they remain today, as magical practices. The neat and clean distinctions we make between science and magic only impede our

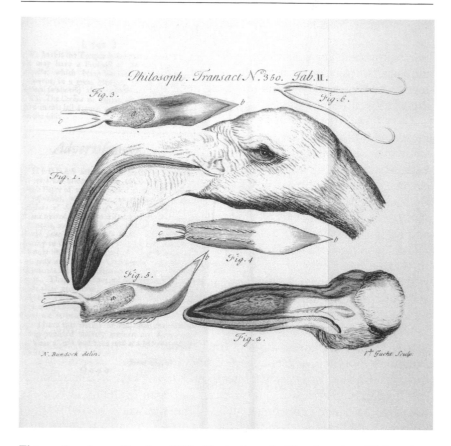

Figure 6. *James Douglas, M.D., Illustration of a Flamingo from* Philosophical Transactions of the Royal Society, *1714.*
This illustration appeared in the same volume of the *Philosophical Transactions of the Royal Society* as the description of diseases in oxen and cattle (Document 16). It brings together the world of imperial exploration and science.
Department of Special Collections, Charles E. Young Research Library, UCLA.

understanding of how early modern natural philosophers imagined nature. Similarly, laying emphasis on the great discoveries of early modern natural philosophy, as important as they were, can obscure the day-to-day interests of the many communities of naturalists. They could discuss agricultural topics or the weather with the same earnestness that they brought to astronomy or optics.

SPREADING THE SCIENTIFIC REVOLUTION

Even with the accomplishments of Galileo, Descartes, Boyle, Newton, and others, popular acceptance of the new science was slow to develop. When it did emerge, it sometimes took fanciful forms. The Dutch natural philosopher, Huygens, used the basic principles articulated by Descartes and, in a flight of imagination that was becoming increasingly frequent in Europe, gave the world a book that foreshadowed science fiction (see Document 13). In *The Celestial Worlds Discovered*, published in 1698, Huygens argued for the existence of life on other planets. If the planets are made of the same matter as the earth, why not inhabit them with the same creatures, human as well as animal? Huygens also used the occasion to champion the new science and to argue for European superiority. Many of the themes that inspired Huygens reappeared over the next few centuries. Some offered liberation and escapism, while others created an intellectual posture that contributed to Western imperialism. In Huygens's day, however, such fantasies were controversial—he willed the book to be published only after his death.

Nothing better indicates the character of day-to-day natural philosophical concerns than the proceedings of one of the many publications that appeared in Europe and eventually America, issued by one of the learned or scientific societies. The *Philosophical Transactions of the Royal Society*—still published today—began in 1665 (Document 16). It printed letters from the learned; the curious; the questioning; those seeking to be informative; and people concerned about epidemics and diseases, strange births, and finding longitude at sea. This journal concentrated on many of the breakthrough discoveries we associate with the Scientific Revolution. In the early modern period, day-to-day concerns about nature that aimed at being accurate, informative, and even original could concern anything and could come from anywhere in the literate world. In societies that were still deeply agricultural, matters that concerned the farm concerned everyone. The official publications of the scientific academies inspired a literature of popularization. Journals such as *The Ladies Diary* (1704–1774) never failed to publish mathematical puzzles and set riddles that required knowledge of natural phenomena. Simple mathematical questions were even set to rhyme: "At London one morning the Sun shining plain / The shadow I found the just length of my cane / As I held it upright; 'twas the tenth day of May, / Now tell me exactly the time of the day."[15]

Many of those who subscribed to such journals and encyclopedias also could be found in polite audiences that witnessed scientific demonstrations and lectures. Barely a town of any size existed in England and the Dutch Republic where such lectures could not be heard. In Newton's lifetime, his friend Jean T. Desaguliers (1683–1744) went everywhere in the English provinces, and on the Continent he spoke in French. His lectures on mechanics drew large audiences in capitals as well as in provincial towns (see Document 17). At the same time, Daniel Fahrenheit (of temperature fame; 1686–1736) not only made thermometers but also lectured on mechanics and optics throughout continental Europe. Outside of Paris, such lecturing was less commonplace in France than in England and Holland. By the 1780s, young manufacturers in towns like Birmingham, Leeds, and Manchester routinely went to lectures on mechanics and sought to apply what they learned to the manufacturing process. Desaguliers also did an English translation of a work by the leading continental follower of Newton, Willem Jacob s' Gravesande (1688–1742) (pronounced schgrav-san-de). This explication of Newtonian mechanics combined mathematics and machines, and with each published edition the machines came to predominate. By the 1790s, vast compendia of the arts and sciences illustrated every conceivable mechanical device and tool, while itinerant lecturers used them in tabletop demonstrations.

But what about the more obtuse ideas and writings that emerged from the Scientific Revolution? How could ordinary people come to understand them? We tend to think about the *Principia* today as largely a work in celestial dynamics. But that is not how contemporaries with practical interests read it—they saw it as a work in mechanics, in the science of local motion. However, few people actually read the book. It was—and is—extremely difficult to understand. Within Newton's lifetime, a small industry arose for the sole purpose of explaining the *Principia*. Dozens of textbooks appeared that broke the mechanics into manageable lessons, often illustrated with machines and not requiring mathematics. Lecturers took to the coffeehouses, halls, and demonstration rooms found not only in large cities such as London but also in every reasonably sized town throughout northern and western Europe. Selling Newtonian mechanics offered the possibility of a career to dozens of well-educated students of natural philosophy. Among the most famous of the first generation was Desaguliers, the official experimenter at the Royal Society of London.

No figure better represents the practical application of the Scientific Revolution than Desaguliers. Two years before Newton published his

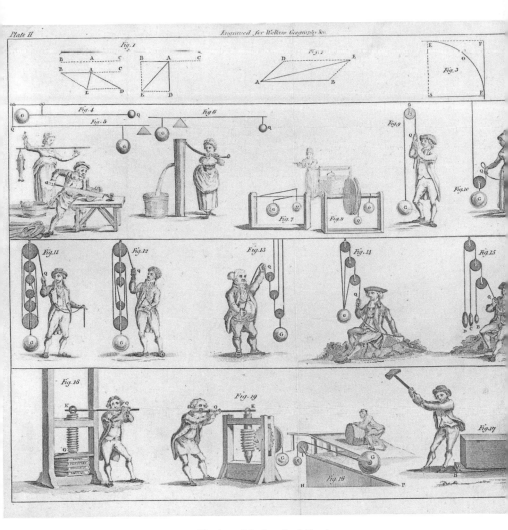

Figure 7. *John Walker, Various Mechanical Devices.*
Drawn on copperplate sometime in the mid- or late eighteenth century in
Britain, the unsigned plate published by John Walker illustrates various methods for using levers, weights, and pulleys in work situations and preludes the
increasing move toward industrialization.

Principia in 1687, King Louis XIV revoked the limited religious free-dom enjoyed by Protestants in his kingdom. Over 150,000 refugees fled France and the Protestant Desaguliers and his parents were among them. After studying at Oxford and being ordained as an Angli-can minister, Desaguliers became an avid experimenter and eventually a member of Newton's inner circle. Before anyone even invented the term, Desaguliers became a civil engineer. He worked on building projects, on the application of steam engines to mines and rivers, on the promotion and dissemination of labor-saving devices such as levers, weights, pulleys, and even simple steam engines. At the Royal Society, he performed electrical experiments and he further demon-strated the existence of the vacuum, a centerpiece of Newton's system of the world. He studied the chemical processes of repulsive and attractive forces, and he related both to the pervasiveness of electric-ity in nature. He became one of a handful of scientific lecturers who created the profession of the itinerant lecturer in natural philosophy. Desaguliers returned to the continent frequently, particularly the Dutch Republic, to lecture on Newtonian science. By 1790, it was pos-sible for John Marshall, a Leeds manufacturer of linen cloth, to study the problems of resistance and velocity, and to learn about the work-ing of steam engines, information he then took onto the factory floor as he sought to increase the speed of bobbins and harness the power of his new steam engines.[16]

Desaguliers illustrates the practical implications to be drawn from an intellectual revolution that in the first instance was conceptual and mathematical. His work in Newtonian mechanics points toward the Industrial Revolution that began first in Britain in the 1780s. Desag-uliers was a new breed of civil engineer. He made his living not as a state servant, like most French engineers, but in the marketplace. He was also a clergyman more occupied as a mechanical engineer than as a pulpit orator. In 1736 William Hogarth engraved a satirical print on "The Sleeping Congregation." Desaguliers was widely said to be the preacher. He may have bored his congregations, but he knew the mar-ketplace. The practical men to whom his text appealed were interested in building canals, moving coal out of mines, and manufacturing things more quickly and cheaply.

Benjamin Franklin (1706–1790) was a direct heir of Desaguliers's concern for utility and application. Indeed in the 1720s, when Franklin lived in London, his best friend was a lodger at the home of Desag-uliers. Franklin's interests ranged from electricity, where he made original contributions by identifying positive and negative charges

Figure 8. *Portrait of Jean Desaguliers, 1743.*
Desaguliers was a new kind of clergyman who was also an engineer.
This item is reproduced by permission of The Huntington Library, San Marino, California.

(see Document 18), to heating stoves. He was an electrical experimenter who inflicted charges on himself to try to understand their strength. He pioneered bifocal glasses, founded state-of-the-art hospitals, and set up voluntary societies where people could hear about science or listen to lectures. He accepted the mechanical philosophy wholeheartedly and saw himself as engaged in solving problems bequeathed by Newton's observations in the *Thirty-first Query to the* OPTICKS. In his support for the new United States, Franklin turned his vision of scientific progress into serving the new republic. No area— from the gulf stream to shipping and navigation to manufacturing— escaped his attention. He became so famous that twenty thousand people attended his funeral in Philadelphia.

First in Britain by the 1780s and then in nineteenth-century continental Europe and North America, a new breed of mechanically and chemically educated entrepreneurs put engineers to work. Armed with the principles of Newtonian mechanics, together they built the first steam-powered factories. By the 1770s in coal fields near Newcastle in the north of England, one of the richest coal regions in Europe, there were over one hundred steam engines operating at ground level and below. This was at a time when no steam engines were used in French coal mines and only about a half dozen were present in the Belgian fields. Steam facilitated the dredging of harbors, the draining of swamps, the mining of coal, the weaving of raw cotton into cloth, and eventually the weaving of linen and wool. Just as had the natural philosophers before them, the engineers and entrepreneurs formed societies and offered lectures and demonstrations aimed first to make themselves, and then their skilled workers, scientifically literate. Through their efforts, steam power became a general-purpose technology that moved from mining and manufacturing to railroads and ships.

Whether at the royal courts or in one of the many formal and informal societies or academies that sprang to life under the impetus of natural inquiries, the practice of natural philosophy benefited enormously from social interactions. There was a small informal philosophical society around Galileo, and Huygens journeyed to Paris from the Dutch Republic to partake in the social life and patronage offered by the French academy. The founding of the *Accademia dei Lincei* in the early 1600s in Florence, the Royal Society in London in 1660, the *Académie des sciences* in Paris in 1666, and the Academy of Sciences in St. Petersburg, Russia, in 1725 establishes dates when strong interest in the new science took hold. Of all the seventeenth-century academies, perhaps the Royal Society of London became the most famous and prestigious. It was entirely private and depended on membership dues. Yet by the time Newton assumed its presidency, men from all over Europe and the American colonies aspired to be named Fellows, and anyone who could put F.R.S. (Fellow of the Royal Society) after his name made a point of doing so.

When in the 1720s the king of Russia, Peter the Great, self-consciously sought to copy the behavior he had observed in Paris and London, science was already largely public, open, and increasingly cosmopolitan. Why did the intensely social configuration of the small society, composed of relative strangers, usually accompanied by some foreign members, become so integral to the growth of Western science? The example of Peter the Great helps to explain this. Peter saw such academies as "nothing if not a society [gathering] of persons who assist each other for the purpose of the carrying out of the sciences." Then, tellingly, he said that experiments needed to be verified in the presence of all members because "in some experiments many times one demands a complete demonstration from another, as, for example, an anatomist of the mechanic, etc." One person could not quite understand what another was trying to say without seeing it demonstrated. The complexity of the natural world required specialization and it, in turn, required social interaction among relative strangers to grasp what needed to be communicated. Thus, though the practice of science was often local, the frequent inclusion of international observers and contacts was also important for demonstrating scientific work.[17]

Something else also happened in these social settings. In the early modern period, habits were put in place that powerfully shaped the self-policing character of scientific inquiry. In effect, quite early in the formation of modern science and long before the creation of the modern laboratory, the doers of natural inquiry operated in groups that could conceivably include those who would become their most vigorous competitors and thus among their most attentive critics. As the late sociologist of science, Pierre Bourdieu, explained, such habits, once institutionalized, have come to mean that scientific work can be assessed through a shared process that aims toward the goal of greater rationality.[18] This cosmopolitan effect helped to set the self-examining character of science as we know it.

The very practices and languages of early modern science thus unwittingly played into the formation of a cosmopolitan experience, at least for men. The boundaries of natural inquiry, as distinct from other forms of learning, were fluid, disciplines were unformed, yet specialization existed. The fluidity of borders between the realms of each specialty—between mechanist and anatomist or between botanist and alchemist—led to social interaction, and so too did experimental demonstration. Inadvertently and slowly, within select groups where interest in nature dominated, cosmopolitan social manners and customs were invented and strengthened. National borders were crossed and, to some degree, social classes as well, because specialized knowledge was constantly being conveyed to those slightly less expert than the conveyor. Nothing was inherently cosmopolitan or open about the practitioners of science themselves. Indeed national rivalries, competition, and social nastiness were commonplace in early modern scientific circles. But natural inquiry, more than any other single new cultural phenomenon of the era—more than reading, or coffeehousing, or clubbing—constantly threw male strangers, and as we saw, a few female ones, into new and sustained social contact over problems that experience or experiments with nature presented. Long before the modern laboratory became inherent in scientific work, group experience, complete with differences bridged but rivalries also enhanced, had become commonplace. This was especially true when medical and alchemical topics came up for discussion. What could be more compelling than the challenge of trying to find medical cures, or the elixir of life, or speculating on the elusive practice of attempting to transmute base metals into gold? The alchemical quest required border crossing, and alchemy offers one of the keys to understanding the emergence of the cosmopolitan within the ethos of science.[19]

To be sure, many factors were at work in shaping a cosmopolitan ethos within early modern science. But if scientific work were to be expanded on, a common ideology and a common vocabulary about nature that could be shared across the borders of Europe were needed. By the mid-seventeenth century, there was no agreement as to what that vocabulary would be. Agreement emerged only gradually, generally by the 1690s. In the seventeenth century, a variety of philosophical languages and practices competed. One was derived from Aristotle and entrenched in the schools and universities. Another was alchemical and associated with a sixteenth-century doctor, Paracelsus (1493–1541), and flourished in private circles and at the courts. The ultimate victor in the struggle to establish a common vocabulary was deemed "mechanical" science and was associated with Galileo, Descartes, and Boyle. Their medium for communication and promotion included print culture, the new learned academies, and some courts. Gradually displacing "forms," "sympathies," or "tendencies" came new words—matter, motion, contact action, vacuum, and attraction. Understanding those terms had first been the privilege of men, but by the mid-eighteenth century women had become consumers of mathematics and science, attending lectures and demonstrations, even forming their own scientific society.

CONCLUSION: THE LONG ROAD TO ACCEPTANCE

Aristotelian science was dethroned gradually. When the future architect of free-market economics Adam Smith (1723–1790) attended Oxford University in 1740, he was horrified to find that in philosophical matters the curriculum was still heavily Aristotelian. His own university in Glasgow was more philosophically modern and he would have had more of an intellectual feast at Cambridge, where Newton had taught and where the new science and its natural philosophy had been ensconced. Had Smith crossed the channel and ventured to the Sorbonne in Paris, he would have also found Aristotle alive and well in the curriculum, with only Descartes offering a serious challenge.

In France, Newtonian science only made deep inroads in the academies after 1750 and largely because, as one scholar puts it, "If Newton finally triumphed in France it was probably over the corpse of the Jesuit Order." In other words, Jesuit teachers who controlled the majority of French colleges had just gotten to the point of embracing Descartes; Newton was just too much to ask. In the 1760s, for a variety of complex political reasons, the Jesuits were expelled from France. The curricula of the schools and universities decisively shifted and the new science, in its Newtonian form, became commonplace although atomism was still controversial at the beginning of the French Revolution in 1789.[20]

As we watch the negative reaction to science in some religious quarters today, we might think about the achievements of the seventeenth and eighteenth centuries. Within deeply Christian Europe, a new understanding of nature unfolded—not without opposition, particularly among Scholastics—and it valorized the empirical, the experimental, the mathematical, and the mechanical. Banished were notions of hidden, unknowable forces in nature, spirits, and demons. Mathematics had once been seen as a practical tool, not the province of philosophers. By the late seventeenth century, it had come to be relevant to everything from predicting life expectancy to calibrating machines. These changes coincided with the discovery of new peoples and continents, which in turn suggested that ancient learning, even recent learning, had to be improved. Religious conflict and intolerance also suggested that new sources of knowledge and authority were urgently needed. Gradually, rationalism and empiricism came to displace tradition and religious dogmatism, and, as a result, modern industrial societies emerged. The new scientific culture when combined with the profit motive and power technology brought into being the industrial age. Its wealth and power turned the West into an imperial and for a time the hegemonic power on our planet.[21]

NOTES

[1]José de Acosta, *Natural and Moral History of the Indies*, trans. Frances M. López-Morillas (Durham, N.C.: Duke University Press, 2002), 20–21.

[2]See Richard G. Lipsey, "Economic Growth Related to Mutually Interdependent Institutions and Technology," http://www.econ.sfu.ca/research/RePEc/sfu/sfudps/dp08-03.pdf. For the quotation comparing Europe with the East, see Jack Goldstone, *Why Europe? The Rise of the West in World History* (New York: McGraw-Hill, 2009), 20. The notion of the paradigm shift belongs to Thomas Kuhn, *The Structure of Scientific Revolutions* (Chicago: University of Chicago Press, 1962). For the various approaches taken to the question, see Steven Shapin, who dwells on Robert Boyle and also argues that there really was no scientific revolution, in his *The Scientific Revolution* (Chicago: University of Chicago Press, 1996); for Betty Jo Dobbs and alchemy, see the essay by her and others in Margaret Osler, ed., *Rethinking the Scientific Revolution* (Cambridge: Cambridge University Press, 2000). For the founding of the university and science at Berlin, see Thomas Albert Howard, *Protestant Theology and the Making of the Modern German University* (Oxford: Oxford University Press, 2006), chap. 3. For the importance of patronage, see Paul A. David, "The Historical Origins of 'Open Science': An Essay on Patronage, Reputation and Common Agency Contracting in the Scientific Revolution," *Capitalism and Society* 3, no. 2 (2008): article 5 For Aristotle, I used *Physics*, trans. Robin Waterfield (New York: Oxford University Press, 1996).

[3]Brian P. Copenhaver and Charles B. Schmidt, *Renaissance Philosophy* (New York: Oxford University Press, 1992).

[4]Francis Suarez, *On the Formal Cause of Substance: Metaphysical Disputation XV*, trans. John Kronen and Jeremiah Reedy; introduction and explanatory notes by John Kronen (Milwaukee: Marquette University Press, 2000), 17–19.

[5]For scholarship on the process of imperial expansion as experienced by the Dutch, see Harold J. Cook, *Matters of Exchange: Commerce, Medicine, and Science in the Dutch Golden Age* (New Haven, Conn.: Yale University Press, 2007). Also quite interesting are Anne Goldgar, *Tulipmania: Money, Honor, and Knowledge in the Dutch Golden Age* (Chicago: University of Chicago Press, 2007), and Julia Adams, *The Familial State: Ruling Families and Merchant Capitalism in Early Modern Europe* (Ithaca, N.Y.: Cornell University Press, 2005). For a fresh and suitably harsh look at the nature of Dutch imperialism in the period and its impact on the visual arts, see Julie Berger Hochstrasser,

Still Life and Trade in the Dutch Golden Age (New Haven, Conn.: Yale University Press, 2007). See also Antonio Barrera-Osorio, *Experiencing Nature: The Spanish American Empire and the Early Scientific Revolution* (Austin: University of Texas Press, 2006); Miguel de Asúa and Roger French, *A New World of Animals: Early Modern Europeans on the Creatures of Iberian America* (Burlington, Vt.: Ashgate, 2005); and, on the new mathematics, see Amir Alexander, *Geometrical Landscapes: The Voyages of Discovery and the Transformation of Mathematical Practice* (Stanford, Calif.: Stanford University Press, 2002). In general, see Joan-Paul Rubiés, *Travel and Ethnology in the Renaissance: South India through European Eyes, 1250–1625* (Cambridge: Cambridge University Press, 2000). And see Francis Bacon, *The New Organon*, ed. Lisa Jardine and Michael Silverthorne (Cambridge: Cambridge University Press, 2000), 93.

[6]Deborah E. Harkness, *The Jewel House: Elizabethan London and the Scientific Revolution* (New Haven, Conn.: Yale University Press, 2007).

[7]Quoted in Jean Dietz Moss, *Novelties in the Heavens: Rhetoric and Science in the Copernican Controversy* (Chicago: University of Chicago Press, 1993), 33.

[8]*Réimpression de l'Ancien Moniteur*, t. 29, 1847, 402–3. Number 1, reprinting the speech given by François de Neufchâteau on 1 Vendémiaire, Year 7, September 26, 1798.

[9]Laura Fermi and Gilberto Bernardini, *Galileo and the Scientific Revolution* (Mineola, N.Y.: Dover Publications, 2003), 85–86.

[10]Scriptural verses relevant to Galileo's trial (from the King James Version of the Bible and the Douay/Rheims Catholic Bible):

Joshua 10 (Verse 13)
[King James Bible]
And the sun stood still, and the moon stayed, until the people had avenged themselves upon their enemies. Is not this written in the book of Jasher? **So the sun stood still in the midst of heaven,** and hasted not to go down about a whole day.

[Catholic Bible]
13 And the sun and the moon stood still, till the people revenged themselves of their enemies. Is not this written in *the book of the just?* **So the sun stood still in the midst of heaven,** and hasted not to go down the space of one day.

Psalm 19 (Verses 1–5)
[King James Bible]
1 The heavens declare the glory of God; and **the firmament sheweth his handywork.**
2 Day unto day uttereth speech, and night unto night sheweth knowledge.
3 There is no speech nor language, where their voice is not heard.
4 Their line is gone out through all the earth, and their words to the end of the world. **In them hath he set a tabernacle for the sun,**
5 **Which is as a bridegroom coming out of his chamber,** and rejoiceth as a strong man to run a race.

Psalm 104 (Verses 1–5)
[King James Bible]
1 Bless the LORD, o my soul. O LORD my God, thou art very great; thou art clothed with honour and majesty.
2 Who coverest thyself with light as with a garment: who stretchest out the heavens like a curtain:
3 Who layeth the beams of his chambers in the waters: who maketh the clouds his chariot: who walketh upon the wings of the wind:
4 Who maketh his angels spirits; his ministers a flaming fire:
5 **Who laid the foundations of the earth, that it should not be removed for ever.**

Isaiah 40 (Verse 22)
[King James Bible]
22 It is he that sitteth upon the circle of the earth, and the inhabitants thereof are as grasshoppers; that stretcheth out the heavens as a curtain, and spreadeth them out as a tent to dwell in.

[Catholic Bible]
22 It is he that sitteth upon the globe of the earth, and the inhabitants thereof are as locusts: he that stretcheth out the heavens as nothing, and spreadeth them out as a tent to dwell in.

A decree of February 19, 1616, summoned Qualifiers of the Holy Office and required them to give their opinion on the two following propositions in Galileo's work on the solar spots. (The assessment was made in Rome, on Wednesday, February 24, 1616.)

Proposition to be assessed:

(1) The sun is the center of the world and wholly immovable from its place.
Assessment: This proposition was unanimously declared "foolish and absurd. philosophically and formally heretical inasmuch as it expressly contradicts the doctrine of the Holy Scripture in many passages, both in their literal meaning and according to the general interpretation of the Holy Fathers and the doctors of theology."
(2) The earth is not the center of the world, nor immovable, but it moves as a whole, also with diurnal motion.
Assessment: This proposition was unanimously declared "deserving of the like censure in philosophy, and as regards theological truth, to be at least erroneous in faith."

[11] Maarten Prak, *The Dutch Republic in the Seventeenth Century* (Cambridge: Cambridge University Press, 2005), 228–31.

[12] William R. Newman, *Atoms and Alchemy: Chymistry and the Experimental Origins of the Scientific Revolution* (Chicago: University of Chicago Press, 2006).

[13] Robert Boyle, *Certain Physiological Essays and Other Tracts . . .* (London: Henry Herringman, 1669), 8.

[14] For Newton's bank records, see Bank of England Archives, London, AC 27/444 Bank Stock Number 21 I-Q Anno 1725–1732, Folio 1105, May 18, 1727, Sir Isaac Newton deceased and with distribution of £1,750 to each of eight people.

[15] *The Ladies Diary* (London: n.p., 1713), Question 30 by A.W.

[16] For the comings and goings of Desaguliers in Whig circles, see British Library MSS ADD 61999 January 1716/17 diary Henry Brydges, second son of Duke of Chandos, vicar at Amersham, Bucks, f. 22 et. seq. On Marshall, see Margaret C. Jacob, "Mechanical Science on the Factory Floor: The Early Industrial Revolution in Leeds," *History of Science* 45 (June 2007): 197–221.

[17] Michael D. Gordin, "The Importance of Being Earnest: The Early St. Petersburg Academy of Sciences," *Isis* 91 (2000): 10.

[18] Pierre Bourdieu, *Science of Science and Reflectivity*, trans. R. Nice (Cambridge: Polity, 2004).

[19] See chapter 2 in Margaret C. Jacob, *Strangers Nowhere in the World: The Rise of Early Modern Cosmopolitanism* (Philadelphia: University of Pennsylvania Press, 2007).

[20] L. W. B. Brockliss, *French Higher Education in the Seventeenth and Eighteenth Centuries: A Cultural History* (Oxford: Oxford University Press, 1987), 366.

[21] Joel Mokyr, *The Gifts of Athena: Historical Origins of the Knowledge Economy* (Princeton, N.J.: Princeton University Press, 2002); also, his "The Intellectual Origins of

Modern Economic Growth," *Journal of Economic History* 45 (2005): 285–351, and his *The Enlightened Economy* (New Haven, Conn.: Yale University Press, 2009). See also http://industrialization.ats.ucla.edu.

PART TWO

The Documents

1

NICOLAUS COPERNICUS

On the Revolutions of the Heavenly Orbs

1543

In 1540, at the urging of his pupil, Georg Joachim Rheticus (1514–1574), Nicolaus Copernicus (1473–1543) agreed to publish De Revolutionibus orbium coelestium *(On the Revolutions of the Heavenly Orbs). The book's dedication to Pope Paul III attests to Copernicus's piety and to his realization that the work would be controversial. In many respects, Copernicus remained a follower of Aristotle. Copernicus worked to eliminate nonuniform circular motions, as these violated Aristotle's understanding of natural motion. Like Aristotle, Copernicus thought that the earth was perfectly spherical; unlike Ptolemy, Copernicus had it moving—in circular motions. He also retained the smaller, uniformly circular epicycles used by Ptolemy to explain why some planets appeared to change their position at certain times of the year.*

To the Most Holy Lord, Pope Paul III. The Preface of Nicolaus Copernicus to the Books of the Revolutions

I may well presume, most Holy Father, that certain people, as soon as they hear that in this book *On the Revolutions of the Heavenly Orbs* I ascribe movement to the earthly globe, will cry out that, holding such views, I should at once be hissed off the stage. For I am not so pleased with my own work that I should fail duly to weigh the judgment which others may pass thereon, and though I know that the speculations of a philosopher are far removed from the judgment of the multitude—for his aim is to seek truth in all things as far as God has permitted human reason so to do—yet I hold that opinions which are quite erroneous should be avoided.

Thinking therefore within myself that to ascribe movement to the earth must indeed seem an absurd performance on my part to those who know that many centuries have consented to the establishment of

Nicolaus Copernicus, *De Revolutionibus: Preface and Book 1*, translated by John F. Dobson (printed originally as *Occasional Notes*). *Royal Astronomical Society* 10 (May 1947): 3–8.

the contrary judgment, namely that the earth is placed immovably as the central point in the middle of the universe, I hesitated long whether, on the one hand, I should give to the light these my commentaries written to prove the earth's motion, or whether, on the other hand, it were better to follow the example of the Pythagoreans[1] and others who were wont to impart their philosophic mysteries only to intimates and friends, and then not in writing but by word of mouth. . . . In my judgment they did so not, as some would have it, through jealousy of sharing their doctrines, but as fearing lest these so noble and hardly won discoveries of the learned should be despised by such as either care not to study aught save for gain, or—if by the encouragement and example of others they are stimulated to philosophic liberal pursuits—yet by reason of the dullness of their wits are in the company of philosophers as drones among bees. Reflecting thus, the thought of the scorn which I had to fear on account of the novelty and incongruity of my theory well-nigh induced me to abandon my project.

These misgivings and actual protests have been overcome by my friends. First among these was Nicolaus Schönberg, cardinal of Capua, a man renowned in every department of learning. Next was one who loved me well, Tiedemann Giese, bishop of Kulm, a devoted student of sacred and all other good literature, who often urged and even importuned me to publish this work which I had kept in store not for nine years only, but to a fourth period of nine years. The same request was made to me by many other eminent and learned men. They urged that I should not, on account of my fears, refuse any longer to contribute the fruits of my labors to the common advantage of those interested in mathematics. They insisted that, though my theory of the earth's movement might at first seem strange, yet it would appear admirable and acceptable when the publication of my elucidatory comments should dispel the mists of paradox. Yielding then to their persuasion I at last permitted my friends to publish that work which they have so long demanded.

That I allow the publication of these my studies may surprise your Holiness the less in that, having been at such travail to attain them, I had already not scrupled to commit to writing my thoughts upon the motion of the earth. How I came to dare to conceive such motion of the earth, contrary to the received opinion of the mathematicians and

---

[1]A secretive Greek sect.

indeed contrary to the impression of the senses, is what your Holiness will rather expect to hear. So I should like your Holiness to know that I was induced to think of a method of computing the motions of the spheres by nothing else than the knowledge that the mathematicians are inconsistent in these investigations.

For, first, the mathematicians are so unsure of the movements of the sun and moon that they cannot even explain or observe the constant length of the seasonal year. Secondly, in determining the motions of these and of the other five planets, they do not even use the same principles and hypotheses as in their proofs of seeming revolutions and motions. So some use only concentric circles, while others eccentrics and epicycles. Yet even by these means they do not completely attain their ends. Those who have relied on concentrics, though they have proven that some different motions can be compounded therefrom, have not thereby been able fully to establish a system which agrees with the phenomena. Those again who have devised eccentric systems, though they appear to have well-nigh established the seeming motions by calculations agreeable to their assumptions, have yet made many admissions which seem to violate the first principle of uniformity in motion. Nor have they been able thereby to discern or deduce the principal thing—namely the shape of the universe and the unchangeable symmetry of its parts. With them it is as though an artist were to gather the hands, feet, head, and other members for his images from diverse models, each part excellently drawn, but not related to a single body, and since they in no way match each other, the result would be monster rather than man. So in the course of their exposition, which the mathematicians call their system . . . we find that they have either omitted some indispensable detail or introduced something foreign and wholly irrelevant. This would of a surety not have been so had they followed fixed principles, for if their hypotheses were not misleading, all inferences based thereon might be surely verified. Though my present assertions are obscure, they will be made clear in due course.

I pondered long upon this uncertainty of mathematical tradition in establishing the motions of the system of the spheres. At last I began to chafe that philosophers could by no means agree on any one certain theory of the mechanism of the universe, wrought for us by a supremely good and orderly creator, though in other respects they investigated with meticulous care the minutest points relating to its orbits. I therefore took pains to read again the works of all the philosophers on whom I could lay hand to seek out whether any of them had ever supposed that the motions of the spheres were other than those demanded by the mathematical schools. I found first in Cicero that Hicetas had realized that the earth moved. Afterwards I found in Plutarch that certain others had held the like opinion. I think fit here to add Plutarch's own words, to make them accessible to all:

> The rest hold the earth to be stationary, but Philolaus the Pythagorean says that she moves around the (central) fire on an oblique circle like the sun and moon. Heraclides of Pontus and Ecphantus the Pythagorean also make the earth to move, not indeed through space but by rotating round her own center as a wheel on an axle from west to east.

Taking advantage of this, I too began to think of the mobility of the earth, and though the opinion seemed absurd, yet knowing now that others before me had been granted freedom to imagine such circles as they chose to explain the phenomena of the stars, I considered that I also might easily be allowed to try whether, by assuming some motion of the earth, sounder explanations than theirs for the revolution of the celestial spheres might so be discovered.

Thus assuming motions, which in my work I ascribe to the earth, by long and frequent observations I have at last discovered that if the motions of the rest of the planets be brought into relation with the circulation of the earth and be reckoned in proportion to the orbit of each planet, not only do their phenomena presently ensue, but the orders and magnitudes of all stars and spheres, nay the heavens themselves, become so bound together that nothing in any part thereof could be moved from its place without producing confusion of all the other parts and of the universe as a whole. . . .

Book One

1. THAT THE UNIVERSE IS SPHERICAL

In the first place we must observe that the universe is spherical. This is either because that figure is the most perfect, as not being articulated but whole and complete in itself, or because it is the most capacious and therefore best suited for that which is to contain and preserve all things, or again because all the perfect parts of it, namely, sun, moon, and stars, are so formed, or because all things tend to assume this shape, as is seen in the case of drops of water and liquid bodies in general if freely formed. No one doubts that such a shape has been assigned to the heavenly bodies.

2. THAT THE EARTH ALSO IS SPHERICAL

The earth also is spherical, since on all sides it inclines toward the center. At first sight, the earth does not appear absolutely spherical because of the mountains and valleys, yet these make but little variation in its general roundness, as appears from what follows. As we pass from any point northward, the North Pole of the daily rotation gradually rises, while the other pole sinks correspondingly and more stars near the North Pole cease to set, while certain stars in the south do not rise. Thus, *Canopus*, invisible in Italy, is visible in Egypt, while the last star of Eridanus, seen in Italy, is unknown in our colder zone. On the other hand, as we go southward, these stars appear higher, while those which are high for us appear lower. Further, the change in altitude of the pole is always proportional to the distance traversed on the earth, which could not be save on a spherical figure. Hence the earth must be finite and spherical.

Furthermore, dwellers in the east do not see eclipses of the sun and moon which occur in the evening here, nor do they in the west see those which occur here in the morning. Yet mid-day eclipses here are seen later in the day by the eastward dwellers, earlier by the westerners. Sailors too have noted that the sea also assumes the same shape, since land invisible from the ship is often sighted from the masthead. On the other hand, if some shining object on the masthead be observed from the shore, it seems gradually to sink as the vessel leaves the land. It is also a sure fact that water free to flow always seeks a lower level, just as earth does, nor does the sea come higher up the shore than the convexity of the earth allows. It therefore follows that land, rising above the level of ocean, is by so much further removed from the center. . . .

4. THAT THE MOTION OF THE HEAVENLY BODIES IS UNIFORM, CIRCULAR, AND PERPETUAL, OR COMPOSED OF CIRCULAR MOTIONS

We now note that the motion of heavenly bodies is circular. Rotation is natural to a sphere and by that very act is its shape expressed. For here we deal with the simplest kind of body, wherein neither beginning nor end may be discerned nor, if it rotate ever in the same place, may the one be distinguished from the other.

Now in the multitude of heavenly bodies various motions occur. Most evident to sense is the diurnal rotation . . . marking day and night. By this motion the whole universe, save earth alone, is thought to glide from east to west. This is the common measure of all motions, since time itself is numbered in days. Next we see other revolutions in contest, as it were, with this daily motion and opposing it from west to east. Such opposing motions are those of sun and moon and the five planets. Of these the sun portions out the year, the moon the month, the common measures of time. In like manner the five planets define each his own independent period.

But these bodies exhibit various differences in their motion. First their axes are not that of the diurnal rotation, but of the Zodiac, which is oblique thereto. Secondly, they do not move uniformly even in their own orbits, for are not sun and moon found now slower, now swifter in their courses? Further, at times the five planets become stationary at one point and another and even go backward. While the sun ever goes forward unswerving on his own course, they wander in diverse ways, straying now southward, now northward. For this reason they are named *planets*. Furthermore, sometimes they approach earth, being then in *perigee*, while at other times receding they are in *apogee*.

Nevertheless, despite these irregularities, we must conclude that the motions of these bodies are ever circular or compounded of circles.[2] For the irregularities themselves are subject to a definite law and recur at stated times, and this could not happen if the motions were not circular, for a circle alone can thus restore the place of a body as it was. So with the sun which, by a compounding of circular motions, brings ever again the changing days and nights and the four seasons of the year. Now therein it must be that diverse motions are conjoined, since a simple celestial body cannot move irregularly in a single orbit. For such irregularity must come of unevenness either in the moving force (whether inherent or acquired) or in the form of the revolving body. Both these alike the mind abhors regarding the most perfectly disposed bodies.

---

[2]Here Copernicus is retaining the epicycles of Ptolemy.

FRANCIS BACON

The Advancement of Learning

1605

Until Francis Bacon (1561–1626) wrote in favor of learning, something we hardly imagine as needing justification, it had been the domain of the clergy at the universities and a few humanists largely attached to court circles in Italy and France. It was associated with pedantry or, worse, learned circles were often seen to be irreligious and rebellious. Writing to the landed and titled, Bacon sought to win them over to learning for its own sake. As a devout Anglican and loyal supporter of court and king, Bacon urged Protestants to study nature as an act of piety. Knowing God's work, nature, was as good as reading God's word, the Bible, for living a pious life. First, Bacon tackled all the objections that have been raised against learning; then he went on to prescribe how it should be done with regard to the study of nature. In Bacon's hands, the study of nature became an act of godliness, a way toward human perfection. Bacon was talking to people whose idea of nature included hunting and horticulture but not a systematic collecting of natural histories of substances and examination to reveal underlying principles. Bacon tried to find natural substances that would prolong life, and he experimented with nitrite and various opiates in the hope of finding longevity.[1]

[At the opening of his treatise, Bacon boldly announces that his purpose is] to have the true testimonies concerning the dignity of learning to be better heard, without the interruption of tacit objections, I think good to deliver it from the discredits and disgraces which it has received, all from ignorance, but ignorance severally disguised, appearing sometimes in the zeal and jealousy of divines,[2] sometimes

---

[1]Lisa Jardine and Alan Stewart, *Hostage to Fortune: The Troubled Life of Francis Bacon* (New York: Hill and Wang, 1998), 501–8.

[2]*Divines* is another term for clergymen in this period.

From Francis Bacon, *The Advancement of Learning*, ed. W. A. Wright (Oxford: Clarendon Press, 1880).

in the severity and arrogancy of politiques,[3] and sometimes in the errors and imperfections of learned men themselves. I hear the former sort say that knowledge is of those things which are to be accepted with great limitation and caution, that the aspiring to overmuch knowledge was the original temptation and sin whereupon ensued the fall of man, that knowledge has in it somewhat of the serpent, and therefore where it enters into a man it makes him swell; . . . Solomon gives a censure, THAT THERE IS NO END OF MAKING BOOKS, AND THAT MUCH READING IS WEARINESS OF THE FLESH . . . AND THAT HE THAT INCREASES KNOWLEDGE . . . INCREASES ANXIETY, [then] St. Paul gives a caveat, THAT WE BE NOT SPOILED THROUGH VAIN PHILOSOPHY, that experience demonstrates how learned men have been archheretics, how learned times have been inclined to atheism, and how the contemplation of second causes derogate from our dependence upon God, who is the first cause.

To discover then the ignorance and error of this opinion, and the misunderstanding in the grounds thereof, it may well appear these men do not observe or consider that it was not the pure knowledge of nature and universality, a knowledge by the light whereof man did give names unto other creatures in paradise, as they were brought before him, according unto their proprieties, which gave the occasion to the fall, but it was the proud knowledge of good and evil, with an intent in man to give law unto himself, and to depend no more upon God's commandments, which was the form of the temptation. Neither is it any quantity of knowledge, how great soever, that can make the mind of man to swell, for nothing can fill, much less extend the soul of man, but God and the contemplation of God, and therefore Solomon, speaking of the two principal senses of inquisition, the eye and the ear, affirms that *the eye is never satisfied with seeing, nor the ear with hearing*; . . . GOD HAS MADE ALL THINGS BEAUTIFUL, OR DECENT, IN THE TRUE RETURN OF THEIR SEASONS. ALSO HE HAS PLACED THE WORLD IN MAN'S HEART, YET CANNOT MAN FIND OUT THE WORK WHICH GOD WORKS FROM THE BEGINNING TO THE END, declaring not obscurely that God has framed the mind of man as a mirror or glass, capable of the image of the universal world, and joyful to receive the impression thereof, as the eye joys to receive light, and not only delighted in beholding the variety of things and vicissitude of times, but raised also to find out and discern the ordinances and decrees, which throughout all those changes are infallibly observed. And although he does insinuate that

[3]*Politiques* is another term for those we would call politicians.

the supreme or summary law of nature, which he calls THE WORK WHICH GOD WORKS FROM THE BEGINNING TO THE END, is not possible to be found out by man, yet that does not derogate from the capacity of the mind but may be referred to the impediments, as of shortness of life, ill conjunction of labors, ill tradition of knowledge over from hand to hand, and many other inconveniences, whereunto the condition of man is subject. For that nothing parcel [no part] of the world is denied to man's inquiry and invention, he does in another place rule over when he says, THE SPIRIT OF MAN IS AS THE LAMP OF GOD, WHEREWITH HE SEARCHES THE INWARDNESS OF ALL SECRETS. If then such be the capacity and receipt of the mind of man, it is manifest that there is no danger at all in the proportion or quantity of knowledge, how large soever, lest it should make it swell or out-compass[4] itself; no, but it is merely the quality of knowledge, which, be it in quantity more or less, if it be taken without the true corrective thereof, has in it some nature of venom or malignity, and some effects of that venom, which is ventosity or swelling. This corrective spice, the mixture whereof makes knowledge so sovereign, is charity, which the apostle immediately adds to the former clause, for so he says, KNOWLEDGE BLOWS UP, BUT CHARITY BUILDS UP, not unlike unto that which he delivers in another place. IF I SPAKE, says he, WITH THE TONGUES OF MEN AND ANGELS, AND HAD NOT CHARITY, IT WERE BUT AS A TINKLING CYMBAL, not but that it is an excellent thing to speak with the tongues of men and angels, but because, if it be severed from charity, and not referred to the good of men and mankind, it has rather a sounding and unworthy glory than a meriting and substantial virtue. And as for that censure of Solomon, concerning the excess of writing and reading books, and the anxiety of spirit which redounds from knowledge, and that admonition of St. Paul, THAT WE BE NOT SEDUCED BY VAIN PHILOSOPHY, let those places be rightly understood, and they do indeed excellently set forth the true bounds and limitations, whereby human knowledge is confined and circumscribed, and yet without any such contracting . . . , but that it may comprehend all the universal nature of things; for these limitations are three. The first, THAT WE DO NOT SO PLACE OUR FELICITY IN KNOWLEDGE, AS WE FORGET OUR MORTALITY; the second, THAT WE MAKE APPLICATION OF OUR KNOWLEDGE, TO GIVE OURSELVES REPOSE AND CONTENTMENT, AND NOT DISTASTE OR REPINING; the third, THAT WE DO NOT PRESUME BY THE CONTEMPLATION OF NATURE TO

[4]Exceed.

ATTAIN TO THE MYSTERIES OF GOD. For as touching the first of these, Solomon does excellently expound himself in another place of the same book, where he says: I SAW WELL THAT KNOWLEDGE RECEDES AS FAR FROM IGNORANCE AS LIGHT DOES FROM DARKNESS, AND THAT THE WISE MAN'S EYES KEEP WATCH IN HIS HEAD, WHEREAS THE FOOL ROUNDS ABOUT IN DARKNESS, BUT WITHAL I LEARNED, THAT THE SAME MORTAL-ITY INVOLVES THEM BOTH. And for the second, certain it is, there is no vexation or anxiety of mind which result from knowledge otherwise than merely by accident; for all knowledge and wonder (which is the seed of knowledge) is an impression of pleasure in itself . . . it deserves to be . . . not lightly passed over. For if any man shall think by view and inquiry into these sensible and material things to attain that light, whereby he may reveal unto himself the nature or will of God, then indeed is he spoiled by vain philosophy. For the contemplation of God's creatures and works produces (having regard to the works and crea-tures themselves) knowledge, but having regard to God, no perfect knowledge, but wonder, which is broken knowledge. . . . And hence it is true that it hath proceeded that diverse great learned men have been heretical while they have sought to fly up to the secrets of the deity by the waxen wings of the senses. And as for the conceit that too much knowledge should incline a man to atheism, and that the igno-rance of second causes should make a more devout dependence upon God, which is the first cause, first, it is good to ask the question which Job asked of his friends: WILL YOU LIE FOR GOD, AS ONE MAN WILL DO FOR ANOTHER, TO GRATIFY HIM? For certain it is that God works noth-ing in nature but by second causes. And if they would have it other-wise believed, it is mere imposture, as it were in favor towards God, and nothing else but to offer to the author of truth the unclean sacri-fice of a lie. But further, it is an assured truth, and a conclusion of experience, that a little or superficial knowledge of philosophy may incline the mind of man to atheism, but a further proceeding therein does bring the mind back again to religion, for in the entrance of phi-losophy, when the second causes, which are next unto the senses, do offer themselves to the mind of man, if it dwell and stay there it may induce some oblivion of the highest cause, but when a man passes on further, and sees the dependence of causes, and the works of provi-dence, then, according to the allegory of the poets, he will easily believe that the highest link of nature's chain must needs be tied to the foot of Jupiter's chair. To conclude therefore, let no man upon a weak conceit of sobriety or an ill-applied moderation think or maintain that a man can search too far, or be too well studied in the book of

God's word, or in the book of God's works, divinity or philosophy. But rather let men endeavor an endless progress or proficience in both, only let men beware that they apply both to charity, and not to swelling, to use, and not to ostentation, and again, that they do not unwisely mingle or confound these learnings together.

[Having established the inherent piety of learning about God's work from the study of nature, Bacon addressed the gentry and aristocracy of his time and took up the myth that learning would weaken their military discipline and their dedication to the active life. He turns to ancient examples to counter that argument, and then asks in effect if his countrymen would go to doctors who are ill-educated.]

And as for the disgraces which learning receives from politics, they be of this nature: that learning does soften men's minds, and makes them more unapt for the honor and exercise of arms, that it does mar and pervert men's dispositions for matters of government and policy, in making them too curious and irresolute by variety of reading, or too peremptory or positive by strictness of rules and axioms, or too immoderate and overweening by reason of the greatness of examples, or too incompatible and differing from the times by reason of the dissimilitude of examples, or at least, that it does divert men's travails from action and business, and brings them to a love of leisure and privateness, and that it does bring into states a relaxation of discipline, while every man is more ready to argue than to obey and execute. . . .

But these, and the like imputations, have rather a countenance of gravity than any ground of justice, for experience does warrant, that both in persons and in times, there has been a meeting and concurrence in learning and arms, flourishing and excelling in the same men and the same ages. For, as for men, there cannot be a better nor the like instance, as of that pair, Alexander the Great and Julius Caesar the dictator, whereof the one was Aristotle's scholar in philosophy, and the other was Cicero's rival in eloquence. Or if any man had rather call for scholars that were great generals, than generals that were great scholars, let him take Epaminondas the Theban, or Xenophon the Athenian, whereof the one was the first that abated the power of Sparta, and the other was the first that made way to the overthrow of the monarchy of Persia. . . .

And for matters of policy and government, that learning should rather hurt, than enable there unto, is a thing very improbable. We see it is accounted an error to commit a natural body to empiric physicians, which commonly have a few pleasing receipts whereupon they are confident and adventurous, but know neither the causes of diseases, nor the complexions of patients, nor peril of accidents, nor the true method of cures. We see it is a like error to rely upon advocates or lawyers, which are only men of practice and not grounded in their books, who are many times easily surprised when matter falls out besides their experience, to the prejudice of the causes they handle. So by like reason it cannot be but a matter of doubtful consequence if states be managed by empiric statesmen, not well mingled with men grounded in learning.

3

FRANCIS BACON

The Great Instauration

1620

In this piece, written fifteen years after his treatise on learning, Bacon continued to fault the learning of his day and urged people to rely on their sensual observations. He further implied that, although the ancients were great thinkers, there were new vistas to conquer because new worlds had been discovered. Only innovation made discovery possible, he argued, and he acknowledged that nature can at times confound the best human efforts to know it. Humility was needed, not disputation for its own sake (a swipe at the Scholastics) or the heavy hand of authority. Bacon spoke in the first person just as Descartes would do in the 1630s, a common literary technique for the exponents of the new science who wanted to show how their own labors had been difficult but rewarding.

Upon the whole, therefore, it seems that men have not been happy hitherto either in the trust which they have placed in others or in their own industry with regard to the sciences, especially as neither the demonstrations nor the experiments as yet known are much to be

Francis Bacon, *The Great Instauration*, ed. J. Spedding et al., vol. 8 (Boston: Taggard & Thompson, 1863).

relied upon. But the universe to the eye of the human understanding is framed like a labyrinth, presenting as it does on every side so many ambiguities of way, such deceitful resemblances of objects and signs, natures so irregular in their lines and so knotted and entangled. And then the way is still to be made by the uncertain light of the sense, sometimes shining out, sometimes clouded over, through the woods of experience and particulars, while those who offer themselves for guides are (as was said) themselves also puzzled, and increase the number of errors and wanderers. In circumstances so difficult neither the natural force of man's judgment nor even any accidental felicity offers any chance of success. No excellence of wit, no repetition of chance experiments, can overcome such difficulties as these. Our steps must be guided by a clue, and the whole way from the very first perception of the senses must be laid out upon a sure plan. Not that I would be understood to mean that nothing whatever has been done in so many ages by so great labors. We have no reason to be ashamed of the discoveries which have been made, and no doubt the ancients proved themselves in everything that turns on wit and abstract meditation, wonderful men. But, as in former ages, when men sailed only by observation of the stars, they could indeed coast along the shores of the old continent or cross a few small and Mediterranean seas, but before the ocean could be traversed and the New World discovered, the use of the mariner's needle, as a more faithful and certain guide, had to be found out. In like manner, the discoveries which have been hitherto made in the arts and sciences are such as might be made by practice, meditation, observation, argumentation—for they lay near to the senses and immediately beneath common notions, but before we can reach the remoter and more hidden parts of nature, it is necessary that a more perfect use and application of the human mind and intellect be introduced.

[Bacon never doubted the necessity for divine guidance and that, although progress was possible it required humility and perseverance.]

For my own part at least, in obedience to the everlasting love of truth, I have committed myself to the uncertainties and difficulties and solitudes of the ways and, relying on the divine assistance, have upheld my mind both against the shocks and embattled ranks of opinion, and against my own private and inward hesitations and scruples, and against the fogs and clouds of nature, and the phantoms flitting about on every side, in the hope of providing at last for the present and future generations guidance more faithful and secure. Wherein if I have made any progress, the way has been opened to me by no other means than the true and legitimate humiliation of the human spirit. For all those who before me have applied themselves to the invention of arts have but cast a glance or two upon facts and examples and experience, and straightway proceeded, as if invention were nothing more than an exercise of thought, to invoke their own spirits to give them oracles. I, on the contrary, dwelling purely and constantly among the facts of nature, withdraw my intellect from them no further than may suffice to let the images and rays of natural objects meet in a point, as they do in the sense of vision, whence it follows that the strength and excellence of the wit has but little to do in the matter. And the same humility which I use in inventing I employ likewise in teaching. For I do not endeavor either by triumphs of confutation, or pleadings of antiquity, or assumption of authority, or even by the veil of obscurity, to invest these inventions of mine with any majesty, which might easily be done by one who sought to give luster to his own name rather than light to other men's minds. I have not sought (I say) nor do I seek either to force or ensnare men's judgments, but I lead them to things themselves and the concordances of things, that they may see for themselves what they have, what they can dispute, what they can add and contribute to the common stock. And for myself, if in anything I have been either too credulous or too little awake and attentive, or if I have fallen off by the way and left the inquiry incomplete, nevertheless I so present these things naked and open, that my errors can be marked and set aside before the mass of knowledge be further infected by them, and it will be easy also for others to continue and carry on my labors. And by these means I suppose that I have established forever a true and lawful marriage between the empirical and the rational faculty, the unkind and ill-starred divorce and separation of which has thrown into confusion all the affairs of the human family.

Wherefore, seeing that these things do not depend upon myself, at the outset of the work I most humbly and fervently pray to God the Father, God the Son, and God the Holy Ghost, that remembering the sorrows of mankind and the pilgrimage of this our life wherein we wear out days few and evil, they will vouchsafe through my hands to endow the human family with new mercies. This likewise I humbly pray that things human may not interfere with things divine and that from the opening of the ways of sense and the increase of natural light there may arise in our minds no incredulity or darkness with regard to the divine mysteries, but rather that the understanding being thereby purified and purged of fancies and vanity, and yet not the less subject and entirely submissive to the divine oracles, may give to faith that which is faith's. Lastly, that knowledge being now discharged of that venom which the serpent infused into it, and which makes the mind of man to swell, we may not be wise above measure and sobriety, but cultivate truth in charity.

[Again, Bacon proclaims that the study of nature is an act of piety.]

4

GALILEO GALILEI

The Starry Messenger

1610

In the following excerpt, Galileo Galilei (1564–1642) put in place a central element of the mechanical philosophy—the assumption of uniformity—that the earth and the planets are made of the same material substance. Such a proclamation required the ability to interpret what he saw using his telescope and to articulate a linkage among theory, method, and instrument.[1] Perhaps Galileo's training in the Renaissance art technique of chiaroscuro—the creation of the illusion of depth by the use of shadows—prepared him to "see" the shadows on the moon for what they actually were—craters, mountains, and so on.[2] Galileo's dedication to theoretical generalization and mathematical expressions extended beyond adherence to the mechanical philosophy. Galileo was convinced that Copernicus had got it right when he argued, on the basis of mathematical

[1]See Yaakov Zik, "Science and Instruments: The Telescope as a Scientific Instrument at the Beginning of the Seventeenth Century," *Perspectives on Science* 9 (2001): 259–84.

[2]Samuel Edgerton, *The Heritage of Giotto's Geometry: Art and Science on the Eve of the Scientific Revolution* (Ithaca, N.Y.: Cornell University Press), 1991.

From Galileo Galilei, *The Sidereal Messenger* (London: Rivingtons, 1880), 10–11, 14–22, 37–38, 68–70.

elegance and simplicity, that the sun must be in the center of the universe. Thus, when Galileo observed the phases of Venus with his telescope, he assumed that they resulted from its rotation around the sun. He also saw that the sun illuminated the moon just as it did the earth.

About ten months ago a report reached my ears that a Dutchman had constructed a telescope,[3] by the aid of which visible objects, although at a great distance from the eye of the observer, were seen distinctly as if near, and some proofs of its most wonderful performances were reported, which some gave credence to, but others contradicted. A few days after, I received confirmation of the report in a letter written from Paris by a noble Frenchman . . . , which finally determined me to give myself up first to inquire into the principle of the telescope, and then to consider the means by which I might compass[4] the invention of a similar instrument, which a little while after I succeeded in doing, through deep study of the theory of refraction, and I prepared a tube, at first of lead, in the ends of which I fitted two glass lenses, both plain on one side, but on the other side one spherically convex, and the other concave. Then bringing my eye to the concave lens I saw objects satisfactorily large and near, for they appeared one-third of the distance off and nine times larger than when they are seen with the natural eye alone. I shortly afterward constructed another telescope with more nicety which magnified objects more than sixty times. At length, by sparing neither labor nor expense, I succeeded in constructing for myself an instrument so superior that objects seen through it appear magnified nearly a thousand times and more than thirty times nearer than if viewed by the natural powers of sight alone.

It would be altogether a waste of time to enumerate the number and importance of the benefits which this instrument may be expected to confer when used by land or sea. But without paying attention to its use for terrestrial objects, I betook myself to observations of the heavenly bodies. . . . After the moon, I frequently observed other heavenly bodies, both fixed stars and planets, with incredible delight; and, when I saw their very great number, I began to consider about a method by which I might be able to measure their distances apart, and at length I found one. . . .

---

[3] There were at least three Dutch instrument makers involved.
[4] Achieve.

Let me speak first of the surface of the moon, which is turned towards us. For the sake of being understood more easily, I distinguish two parts in it, which I call respectively the brighter and the darker. The brighter part seems to surround and pervade the whole hemisphere, but the darker part, like a sort of cloud, discolors the moon's surface and makes it appear covered with spots. Now these spots, as they are somewhat dark and of considerable size, are plain to every one, and every age has seen them, wherefore I shall call them *great* or *ancient* spots to distinguish them from other spots, smaller in size but so thickly scattered that they sprinkle the whole surface of the moon, but especially the brighter portion of it. These spots have never been observed by any one before me, and from my observations of them, often repeated, I have been led to that opinion which I have expressed, namely, that I feel sure that the surface of the moon is not perfectly smooth, free from inequalities and exactly spherical, as a large school of philosophers considers with regard to the moon and the other heavenly bodies, but that, on the contrary, it is full of inequalities, uneven, full of hollows and protuberances, just like the surface of the earth itself, which is varied everywhere by lofty mountains and deep valleys.

The appearances from which we may gather these conclusions are of the following nature: On the fourth or fifth day after new-moon, when the moon presents itself to us with bright horns, the boundary which divides the part in shadow from the enlightened part does not extend continuously in an ellipse, as would happen in the case of a perfectly spherical body, but it is marked out by an irregular, uneven, and very wavy line, as represented in the figure given, for several bright excrescences, as they may be called, extend beyond the boundary of light and shadow into the dark part, and on the other hand pieces of shadow encroach upon the light. Nay, even a great quantity of small blackish spots, altogether separated from the dark part, sprinkle everywhere almost the whole space which is at the time flooded with the sun's light, with the exception of that part alone which is occupied by the great and ancient spots. I have noticed that the small spots just mentioned have this common characteristic always and in every case, that they have the dark part towards the sun's position, and on the side away from the sun they have brighter boundaries, as if they were crowned with shining summits. Now we have an appearance quite similar on the earth about sunrise when we behold the valleys, not yet flooded with light, but the mountains surrounding them on the side opposite to the sun already ablaze with the splendor of his beams, and just as the shadows in the hollows of the earth diminish in size as the sun rises higher, so also these spots on the moon lose their blackness as the illuminated part grows larger and larger.... The grandeur, however, of such prominences and depressions in the moon seems to surpass both in magnitude and extent the ruggedness of the earth's surface, as I shall hereafter show....

Now the great spots of the moon observed at the same time are not seen to be at all similarly broken or full of depressions and prominences, but rather to be even and uniform, for only here and there some spaces, rather brighter than the rest, crop up, so that if any one wishes to revive the old opinion of the Pythagoreans, that the moon is another earth, so to say, the brighter portion may very fitly represent the surface of the land and the darker the expanse of water. Indeed, I have never doubted that if the sphere of the earth were seen from a distance, when flooded with the sun's rays, that part of the surface which is land would present itself to view as brighter, and that which is water as darker in comparison....

There is one other point which I must on no account forget, which I have noticed and rather wondered at. It is this:—The middle of the moon, as it seems, is occupied by a certain cavity larger than all the rest, and in shape perfectly round. I have looked at this depression near both the first and third quarters, and I have represented it as well as I can in the second illustration already given.[5] It produces the same appearance as to effects of light and shade as a tract like Bohemia would produce on the earth, if it were shut in on all sides by very lofty mountains arranged on the circumference of a perfect circle, for the tract in the moon is walled in with peaks of such enormous height that the furthest side adjacent to the dark portion of the moon is seen bathed in sunlight before the boundary between light and shade reaches halfway across the circular space....

By very many arguments and experimental proofs, there is shown to be a very strong reflection of the sun's light from the earth for the benefit of those who urge that the earth must be separated from the starry host, chiefly for the reason that it has neither motion nor light, for I will prove that the earth has motion, and surpasses the moon in brightness, and is not the place where the dull refuse of the universe has settled down, and I will support my demonstration by a thousand arguments taken from natural phenomena....

[5]In an earlier illustration, Galileo attempts to reproduce a deep crater on the surface of the moon.

I have now finished my brief account of the observations which I have thus far made with regard to the moon, the fixed stars, and the galaxy. There remains the matter, which seems to me to deserve to be considered the most important in this work, namely, that I should disclose and publish to the world the occasion of discovering and observing four PLANETS, never seen from the very beginning of the world up to our own times, their positions, and the observations made during the last two months about their movements and their changes of magnitude, and I summon all astronomers to apply themselves to examine and determine their periodic times, which it has not been permitted me to achieve up to this day, owing to the restriction of my time. I give them warning however again, so that they may not approach such an inquiry to no purpose, that they will want a very accurate telescope, and such as I have described in the beginning of this account. . . .

We have a notable and splendid argument to remove the scruples of those who can tolerate the revolution of the planets round the sun in the Copernican system, yet are so disturbed by the motion of one moon about the earth, while both accomplish an orbit of a year's length about the sun, that they consider that this theory of the constitution of the universe must be upset as impossible, for now we have not one planet only revolving about another while both traverse a vast orbit about the sun, but our sense of sight presents to us four satellites circling about Jupiter, like the moon about the earth, while the whole system travels over a mighty orbit about the sun in the space of twelve years.

5

WILLIAM HARVEY

On the Motion of the Heart and Blood in Animals

1628

William Harvey (1578–1657) trained in medicine and anatomy at Padua, and that meant learning the doctrines of Galen, who largely followed Aristotle. Harvey used both authors and believed himself to be operating in their tradition when he did his anatomical work using, as was the custom, live dogs so that the flow of blood could be observed as it was happening. He is not being experimental as much as he is using observation to record what he sees and to argue—using logic—that blood circulates. He realized that his work was subject to criticism because it induced trauma, and vivisection necessarily put the animal into an unnatural condition. Thus he argues his points, stating over and over again that there is no other explanation for what can be seen under these conditions than circulation of the blood. Note the opening reference to the heart as the sun at the center, signaling that he has accepted the Copernican innovation. The royalist sentiments of his opening dedication were probably heartfelt as he was a member of the faculty of London's Royal College of Physicians.

Letter to the King and Dedication

To the Most Illustrious and Indomitable Prince Charles, King of Great Britain, France, and Ireland, Defender of the Faith

Most Illustrious Prince!

The heart of creatures is the foundation of their life, the sovereign of everything within them, the sun of their microcosm, that upon which all growth depends, from which all power proceeds. Likewise the king is the foundation of his kingdom, the sun of the world around him, the heart of the commonwealth, the fountain whence all power, all grace does flow. What I have here written of the motions of the

From *Scientific Papers: Physiology, Medicine, Surgery, Geology with Introductions, Notes and Illustrations* (New York: Collier, 1910).

heart I am the more emboldened to present to Your Majesty, according to the custom of the present age, because almost all things human are done after human examples, and many things in a king are after the pattern of the heart. The knowledge of his heart, therefore, will not be useless to a prince, as embracing a kind of divine example of his functions, — and it has still been usual with men to compare small things with great. Here, at all events, best of princes, placed as you are on the pinnacle of human affairs, you may at once contemplate the prime mover in the body of man, and the emblem of your own sovereign power. Accept therefore, with your accustomed clemency, I most humbly beseech you, illustrious prince, this, my new treatise on the heart; you, who are yourself the new light of this age, and indeed its very heart; a prince abounding in virtue and in grace, and to whom we gladly refer all the blessings which England enjoys, all the pleasure we have in our lives.

Your Majesty's most devoted servant, William Harvey.

Prefatory Remarks

As we are about to discuss the motion, action, and use of the heart and arteries, it is imperative on us first to state what has been thought of these things by others in their writings, and what has been held by the vulgar and by tradition, in order that what is true may be confirmed, and what is false set right by dissection, multiplied experience, and accurate observation.

Almost all anatomists, physicians, and philosophers up to the present time have supposed, with Galen, that the object of the pulse was the same as that of respiration, and only differed in one particular, this being conceived to depend on the animal, the respiration on the vital faculty, the two, in all other respects, whether with reference to purpose or to motion, comporting themselves alike. Whence it is affirmed, as by Hieronymus Fabricius of Aquapendente (1537–1619), in his book on "Respiration,"[1] which has lately appeared, that as the pulsation of the heart and arteries does not suffice for the ventilation and refrigeration of the blood, therefore were the lungs fashioned to surround the heart. From this it appears that whatever has hitherto been said upon the systole and diastole, or on the motion of the heart and arteries, has been said with especial reference to the lungs.

---

[1] An Italian anatomist and surgeon who tutored Harvey at Padua University.

But as the structure and movements of the heart differ from those of the lungs, and the motions of the arteries from those of the chest, so it seems likely that other ends and offices will thence arise, and that the pulsations and uses of the heart, likewise of the arteries, will differ in many respects from the workshop of the spirits, and that the arteries contain and transmit them, denying, however . . . that the lungs can either make or contain spirits. They then assert, with Galen . . . that it is the blood, not spirits, which is contained in the arteries.

These opinions are seen to be so incongruous and mutually subversive, that every one of them is justly brought under suspicion. That it is blood and blood alone which is contained in the arteries is made manifest by the experiment of Galen . . . , for from a single divided artery, as Galen himself affirms in more than one place, the whole of the blood may be withdrawn in the course of half an hour or less. The experiment of Galen alluded to is this: "If you include a portion of an artery between two ligatures, and slit it open lengthwise you will find nothing but blood,"[2] and thus he proves that the arteries contain only blood. And we too may be permitted to proceed by a like train of reasoning: If we find the same blood in the arteries as in the veins, after having tied them in the same way, as I have myself repeatedly ascertained, both in the dead body and in living animals, we may fairly conclude that the arteries contain the same blood as the veins, and nothing but the same blood. Some, while they attempt to lessen the difficulty, affirm that the blood is spirituous and arterious, and virtually concede that the office of the arteries is to carry blood from the heart into the whole of the body, and that they are therefore filled with blood, for spirituous blood is not the less blood on that account. And no one denies the blood as such, even the portion of it which flows in the veins, is imbued with spirits. But if that portion of it which is contained in the arteries be richer in spirits, it is still to be believed that these spirits are inseparable from the blood, like those in the veins; that the blood and spirits constitute one body (like whey and butter in milk, or heat in hot water), with which the arteries are charged, and for the distribution of which from the heart they are provided. This body is nothing else than blood. But if this blood be said to be drawn from the heart into the arteries by the diastole of these vessels, it is then assumed that the arteries by their distension are filled with blood, and not by ambient air. . . . I have never performed this experi-

---

[2] Harvey is quoting from Galen, *On the Natural Faculties*, ca. 170 (CE).

ment of Galen's nor do I think that it could very well be performed in the living body, on account of the profuse flow of blood that would take place from the vessel that was operated on, neither would the tube effectually close the wound in the vessel without a ligature, and I cannot doubt but that the blood would be found to flow out between the tube and the vessel. Still Galen appears by this experiment to prove both that the pulsative property extends from the heart by the walls of the arteries, and that the arteries, while they dilate, are filled by that pulsific force, because they expand like bellows, and do not dilate as if they are filled like skins. But the contrary is obvious in arteriotomy and in wounds, for the blood spurting from the arteries escapes with force, now farther, now not so far, alternately, or in jets, and the jet always takes place with the diastole of the artery, never with the systole. By which it clearly appears that the artery is dilated with the impulse of the blood, for of itself it would not throw the blood to such a distance and while it was dilating; it ought rather to draw air into its cavity through the wound, were those things true that are commonly stated concerning the uses of the arteries. Do not let the thickness of the arterial tunics impose upon us and lead us to conclude that the pulsative property proceeds along them from the heart. For in several animals the arteries do not apparently differ from the veins, and in extreme parts of the body where the arteries are minutely subdivided, as in the brain, the hand, etc., no one could distinguish the arteries from the veins by the dissimilar characters of their coats: the tunics of both are identical. And then, in the aneurysm proceeding from a wounded or eroded artery, the pulsation is precisely the same as in the other arteries, and yet it has no proper arterial covering. . . .

Nor let any one imagine that the uses of the pulse and the respiration are the same, because, under the influences of the same causes, such as running, anger, the warm bath, or any other heating thing, as Galen says, they become more frequent and forcible together. For not only is experience in opposition to this idea, though Galen endeavors to explain it away, when we see that with excessive repletion the pulse beats more forcibly, while the respiration is diminished in amount; but in young persons the pulse is quick, while respiration is slow. So it is also in alarm, and amid care, and under anxiety of mind; sometimes, too, in fevers, the pulse is rapid, but the respiration is slower than usual.

These and other objections of the same kind may be urged against the opinions mentioned. Nor are the views that are entertained of the offices and pulse of the heart perhaps less bound up with great and most inextricable difficulties. The heart, it is vulgarly said, is the fountain and workshop of the vital spirits, the center from which life is dispensed to the several parts of the body. Yet it is denied that the right ventricle makes spirits, which is rather held to supply nourishment to the lungs. For these reasons it is maintained that fishes are without any right ventricle (and indeed every animal wants a right ventricle which is unfurnished with lungs), and that the right ventricle is present solely for the sake of the lungs.

1. Why, I ask, when we see that the structure of both ventricles is almost identical, there being the same apparatus of fibers, and braces, and valves, and vessels, and auricles, and both in the same way in our dissections are found to be filled up with blood similarly black in color, and coagulated—why, I say, should their uses be imagined to be different, when the action, motion, and pulse of both are the same? If the three three-pointed valves placed at the entrance into the right ventricle prove obstacles to the reflux of the blood into the vena cava, and if the three semilunar valves which are situated at the commencement of the pulmonary artery be there, that they may prevent the return of the blood into the ventricle; why, when we find similar structures in connection with the left ventricle, should we deny that they are there for the same end, of preventing here the egress, there the regurgitation, of the blood?

2. And when we have these structures, in points of size, form, and situation, almost in every respect the same in the left as in the right ventricle, why should it be said that things are arranged in the former for the egress and regress of spirits, and in the latter or right ventricle, for the blood? The same arrangement cannot be held fitted to favor or impede the motion of the blood and of spirits indifferently.

3. And when we observe that the passages and vessels are severally in relation to one another in point of size, viz., the pulmonary artery to the pulmonary veins, why should the one be destined to a private purpose, that of furnishing the lungs, the other to a public function?

4. And how is it probable . . . that such a quantity of blood should be required for the nutrition of the lungs, the vessel that leads to them, the vena arteriosa or pulmonary artery being of greater capacity than both the crural veins?

5. And I ask, as the lungs are so close at hand and in continual motion, and the vessel that supplies them is of such dimensions, what is the use or meaning of this pulse of the right ventricle? and why was nature reduced to the necessity of adding another ventricle for the sole purpose of nourishing the lungs?

When it is said that the left ventricle draws matter out of the lungs and the right bosom of the heart to make spirits, that is to say air and blood, from the lungs and right sinuses of the heart, and in like manner sends spirituous blood into the aorta, drawing . . . vapors from there and sending them by the pulmonary vein into the lungs, whence spirits are at the same time obtained for transmission into the aorta, I ask how and by what means is the separation effected? And how comes it that spirits and vapors can pass hither and thither without admixture or confusion? If the mitral cuspidate valves do not prevent the egress of vapors to the lungs, how should they oppose the escape of air? And how should the half-moon portals hinder the regress of spirits from the aorta upon each supervening diastole of the heart? Above all, how can they say that the spirituous blood is sent from the pulmonary veins by the left ventricle into the lungs without any obstacle to its passage from the mitral valves, when they have previously asserted that the air entered by the same vessel from the lungs into the left ventricle, and have brought forward these same mitral valves as obstacles to its retrogression? Good God! how should the mitral valves prevent the regurgitation of air and not of blood?

6

RENÉ DESCARTES
Discourse on Method
1637

René Descartes (1596–1650) moved to the religiously tolerant Dutch Republic following Galileo's trial for heresy, worried that he too might be seen as a heretic by the Catholic Church. His anxiety clearly shapes the cautious tone of Discourse on Method *(1637). Over and over again he makes clear that he does not want to reform the state, or even society at large. He believes deeply in God and in the immortality of the soul. His mission concerns the human mind alone, and his metaphor about the city makes clear his social and political conservatism. It also reflects his preference for the more modern cities of the Dutch Republic and not their medieval predecessors. Descartes is not trying to tear any institution apart; he wishes only to reform how we educate ourselves. In principle, anyone possessed of the ability to reason can follow Descartes' call for the reform of learning as revealed in the* Discourse.

Part One

Good sense is, of all things among men, the most equally distributed, for everyone believes himself so well provided with it that even those who are the most difficult to please in everything else do not usually desire a larger measure of this quality than they already have. It is not likely that they are deceived in this. It indicates rather that the power of judging well, and of distinguishing the true from the false, what is properly called good sense or reason, is by nature equal in all men. . . . For it is not enough to have a vigorous mind, but the main thing is to apply it well. . . .

As for myself, I have never presumed my mind to be in any way more perfect than that of the vast majority of humankind; often I have even wished that I were equal to some others and have as quick a wit,

From René Descartes, *Discourse de la méthode pour bien conduire sa raison et chercher la varité dans les sciences* (Leiden: I. Maire, 1637). Translated from the original by Margaret C. Jacob.

or be as clear and distinct in imagination, or be as ample and ready of memory. . . .

I will not hesitate, however, to avow my belief that it has been my singular good fortune to have very early in life fallen into certain paths that have led me to considerations and maxims from which I have formed a method by which it seems to me that I have the means to increase my knowledge by degrees and to elevate it little by little to the highest point which the mediocrity of my talents and the short duration of my life will permit me to reach. For I have already reaped from it such fruits that, although, as far as the judgments that I make about myself are concerned, I always try to think diffidently and not be presumptuous, and although when I look with the eye of a philosopher at the various courses and pursuits of humankind at large, I scarcely find one that does not appear vain and useless; nevertheless, I derive the highest satisfaction from the progress I conceive myself to have already made in the search after truth, and entertain such hopes for the future that if among the occupations of men purely as men, there is one of them that be surely good and important, I dare to believe that is the one that I have chosen. . . .

I shall be glad to reveal in this discourse what are the paths that I have followed, and thus to represent my life in it as in a picture, so that everyone might judge of it for himself. . . . My aim here is thus not to teach the method that everyone ought to follow in order to conduct his reason correctly, but only to reveal how I have tried to conduct my own. Those who get involved in giving precepts must esteem themselves more capable than those to whom they are giving them. . . . I hope that it will be useful to some without being harmful to anyone, and that all will be grateful to me for my candor.

I have been brought up on books from my childhood, and as I was persuaded that by their help a clear and certain knowledge of all that is useful in life might be acquired, I had an extreme desire to learn from them. But as soon as I had finished the entire course of study, at the close of which one is normally admitted into the ranks of the learned, I completely changed my opinion. For I found myself so encumbered by doubts and errors that it seemed to me I had advanced no further in all my attempts at learning than the discovery at every turn of my own ignorance. And yet I was studying at one of the most famous schools in Europe, where I thought that there must be learned men if there were any of them anywhere on earth. I had been taught all that others learned there, and not contented with the sciences actually taught us, in addition I read all the books I had been able to get my hands on . . . ones . . . most curious and most rare. . . .

I still continued, however, to value the exercises studied in the schools. . . . The reading of all good books is like a conversation with the most upright people of ages past . . . [and] the writings that are very useful [include] theology [which] teaches one how to gain heaven; . . . philosophy gives one the means to speak plausibly about all things and to make oneself admired by the less learned; . . . jurisprudence, medicine, and the other science bring honors and riches to those who cultivate them, and finally, it is good to have examined them all, even the most superstitious and the most false, in order to know their true value and to guard against being deceived by them.

. . . . It is good to know something of the customs of different peoples, in order to judge more soundly our own customs, and so that we might not think that all that is contrary to our own ways be ridiculous and contrary to reason, as those who have seen nothing have the habit of doing. . . .

I was especially pleased with mathematics, on account of the certitude and evidence of its reasoning; but I did not as yet notice its true use, and thinking that it only served the mechanical arts, I was astonished thereby that its foundations being so firm and so solid that no one had built anything lofty upon them. On the other hand, I compared the writings of the ancient pagans that deal with morals and found them to be towering and magnificent palaces with no better foundation than sand and mud. They extol the virtues so highly and make them appear more valuable than everything in the world. . . .

I revered our theology and aspired, as much as anyone else, to reach heaven, but I came to understand that the way is not less open to the most ignorant than to the most learned, and that the revealed truths that guide us there are beyond our comprehension, I would not have dared to submit them to my feeble reasoning, and I thought that in order to undertake to examine them and to succeed in it, one would need to have some extraordinary help from heaven and need to be more than a mere man.

Of philosophy I will say nothing, except that when I saw that it had been cultivated for many ages by the most distinguished men, and that yet there is not a simple matter within its sphere which is not still in dispute, and nothing therefore that is above doubt, I did not presume to imagine that my success would be greater in it than that of others . . . and finally for the false teachings, I thought that I already knew what they were worth well enough in order no longer to be deceived, neither by the promises of the alchemists, nor the predictions of an astrologer, nor by the deceptions of a magician, nor by the tricks and boasts of any of those who make a profession of knowing more than they do know.

That is why, as soon as my age permitted me to emerge from the control of my teachers, I entirely abandoned the study of letters. . . . I spent the rest of my youth traveling, seeing courts and armies, associating with people of different temperaments and circumstances, gathering various experiences, testing myself. . . . And I always had an extreme desire to learn to distinguish the true from the false, in order to see clearly in my actions and to proceed with confidence in this life. . . . Little by little I delivered myself from many errors that can obscure our natural light and render us less capable of listening to reason. After I had spent some years in studying in the book of the world and trying to acquire some experience, I one day made the resolution to study within myself, too, and to use all the powers of my mind in choosing the paths that I should follow, an undertaking which was accompanied with greater success than it would have been had I never quit my country or my books.

Part Two

I was then in Germany. . . . I remained the whole day shut up alone in a stove-heated room, where I had total leisure to converse with myself about my thoughts. Of these, one of the first was that . . . there is often not as much perfection in works composed of several pieces and made by the hands of diverse masters as in those on which one master alone has worked. Thus one sees that buildings built by a single architect . . . are usually more beautiful and better arranged than those which many have tried to patch together by using old walls built for different purposes. Thus those ancient cities which have grown from mere villages and have become with the passage of time great towns are ordinarily so badly put together, compared with those regular places which an engineer traces out on a plain according to his fantasy. . . . And thus I thought that the sciences found in books . . . having been composed and enlarged little by little from the opinions of many different persons, are not at all so close to the truth as are the simple reasonings that a man of good sense can naturally perform concerning the things that present themselves. . . .

It is true that we do not see anyone destroy all the houses of a city for the sole purpose of redoing them in a different fashion . . . , but it often happens that a private individual takes down his own house with a view of erecting it anew. . . . By this example I was persuaded that it would truly not be at all plausible that an individual were to have a plan to reform a state by changing everything in it from the foundations up and by overturning it in order to set it up again, nor even also to reform the body of the sciences or the order of teaching them established in the schools; but as for the opinions that up to that time I had embraced, I thought that I could do no better than resolve at once to sweep them entirely away, that I might afterwards replace them either by other, better ones, or even by the same ones, when I would have subjected them to the scrutiny of reason. I firmly believed that in this way I should much better succeed in the conduct of my life than if I were to build only on old foundations and to rely only on the principles which in my youth I had taken on trust.

That is why I cannot in any way approve of those turbulent and restless spirits who, being neither by their birth nor by their fortune called to take part in the management of public affairs, never cease to have an idea for some new reformation in this area. And if I thought that this tract contained anything that might justify the suspicion that I engaged in such folly, I would be very sorry to have allowed it to be published. I have never contemplated anything higher than the reformation of my own opinions, basing them wholly on a foundation that is my own. . . . The single-minded design to strip one's self of all past beliefs ought not to be taken by every one.

I resolved to proceed slowly and with much circumspection that if I did not advance far, I would at least guard against falling. I also did not want to begin to reject entirely any of the opinions that had once been introduced without reason until I had first spent enough time in devising a plan for the work I was undertaking and on seeking the true method for arriving at the knowledge of all things of which my mind would be capable. . . .

I believed that the four following principles would prove perfectly sufficient for me, provided I took the firm and unwavering resolution never in a single instance to fail in observing them.

The first was never to accept anything for true which I did not clearly know to be such, that is, carefully avoiding being precipitous or prejudicial, and to include in my judgments nothing more than that which would present itself to my mind so clearly and so distinctly that I were to have no occasion to put it in doubt.

The second, to divide each of the difficulties that I would examine into as many parts as would be possible and as would be required in order better to resolve them.

The third, to conduct my thoughts in such an orderly manner that by beginning with objects that are the simplest and easiest to know, I might ascend little by little—as it were step by step—to the knowledge of the more complex, and supposing an order even among those which do not naturally precede one another.

And last, in every case to make enumerations so complete, and reviews so general, that I might be assured that nothing was omitted.

The long chains of simple and easy reasonings by means of which geometers are accustomed to reach the conclusions of their most difficult demonstrations, had led me to imagine that all things, to the knowledge of which man is competent, follow from each other in the same fashion, and that, provided only that one abstain from accepting any of them as true that not be . . . there can be none so remote that one cannot finally reach them, nor so hidden that one cannot discover them. . . .

Part Three

Now before starting to rebuild your house, it is not enough simply to pull it down, to make provision for materials and architects, or to train oneself in architecture . . . , it is also necessary to be provided with some other place which we may live comfortably during the work on the first one. . . . That I might not be prevented from living henceforth in the greatest possible happiness I formed a provisional morality, which consisted of three or four maxims which I would gladly like to share with you.

The first was to obey the laws and customs of my country, holding firmly to the faith in which by the grace of God, I had been instructed from my childhood, and governing myself in every other thing according to the most moderate opinions, and those furthest removed from excess. . . . Also, amid many opinions held in equal repute, I chose always the most moderate, as much for the reason that these are always the most convenient for practice, and probably the best (for all excess is generally vicious). . . .

My second maxim was to be as firm and resolute in my actions as I was able, and not to adhere less steadfastly to the most doubtful opinions, when once adopted, than if they had been highly certain; imitating in this the example of travelers who, when they have lost their way in a forest, ought not to wander from side to side, far less remain in one place, but proceed constantly towards the same side in as straight a line as possible, without changing their direction for slight reasons, although perhaps it might be chance alone that at first determined the direction selected. . . .

My third maxim was to try always to master myself rather than fortune, and change my desires rather than the order of the world, and generally, to accustom myself to believe that there is nothing that be entirely within our power but our thoughts so that when we have done our best with respect to things external to us, all that which is lacking for us to succeed is, in regard to us, absolutely impossible. This alone, I thought, would be sufficient to prevent me from desiring for the future anything which I could not obtain, and thus render me content. For our will tending naturally to desire nothing but those things which our understanding represents to it in some fashion as possible, it is certain that, if we consider all the goods that are outside us as equally beyond our power, we shall no more regret the absence of such goods as seem due to our birth, when deprived of them without any fault of ours, than our not possessing the kingdoms of China or Mexico, and thus making a virtue out of a necessity, as one says, we shall no more desire to be healthy, being sick, or to be free, being in prison. . . . I confess there is need of prolonged discipline and frequently repeated meditation to accustom the mind to view all in this light. . . .

Finally concluding this morality, I took it upon myself to do a review of the various occupations that men have in this life, in order to try to choose the best one. . . . I thought that I could not do better than to continue in that very one in which I found myself, that is to say, than to spend all my life in cultivating my reason, and in advancing, as far as I could, in the knowledge of truth, following the method that I had prescribed to myself. . . . For since God has endowed each of us with some light of reason by which to distinguish truth from error, I could not have believed that I ought for a single moment to rest satisfied with the opinions of another, unless I had resolved to exercise my own judgment in examining these whenever I should be duly qualified for the task. . . . It is now exactly eight years since this desire constrained me to remove from all those places where interruption from any of my acquaintances was possible, and betake myself to this country [the Netherlands], in which the long duration of the war has led to the establishment of such discipline . . . and where in the midst of a great crowd actively engaged in business, and more careful of their own affairs than curious about those of others, I have been able to live without being deprived of any of the conveniences to be had in the most populous cities, and yet as solitary and retired as in the most remote deserts.

Part Four

I do not know whether I should tell you about the first meditations that I had made; they are so metaphysical and so unusual that perhaps they will not be to the taste of everyone. And yet, in order that one might be able to judge whether the foundations that I have laid are sufficiently firm, I find myself in some fashion constrained to talk about them. For a long time, I had noticed that in matters of morals it is sometimes necessary to follow opinions that one knows to be quite uncertain—all the same as if they were indubitable . . . , but because I then desired to devote myself solely to the search for the truth, I thought that it was necessary that . . . I were to reject as absolutely false all that in which I could imagine the least doubt, in order to see whether there would remain, after that, something in my beliefs that were entirely undoubtable. . . . And finally, considering that all the same thought that we have when we are awake can also come to us when we are asleep, without there being any of them at that time that be true, I resolved to feign that all the things that had ever entered my mind were no more true than the illusions of my dreams. But immediately afterward, I took note that, while I wanted thus to think that everything was false, it necessarily had to be that I, who was thinking this, were something. And noticing that this truth—*I think, therefore I am*—was so firm and so assured that all the most extravagant suppositions of the skeptics were not capable of shaking it, I judged that I could accept it, without scruple, as the first principle of the philosophy that I was seeking.

In the next place, paying attention to what I doubted, and seeing that I could feign that I had nobody, and that there was no world, nor any place where I were, but that I could not feign . . . that I was not at all, and seeing that on the contrary from the very fact that I thought of doubting the truth of other things, it followed very evidently and very certainly that I was . . . I knew, from this, that I was a substance the whole essence or nature of which is only to think, and which in order to be, does not need of any place, and does not depend on any material thing. Thus this "I," that is to say, the soul through which I am that which I am, is entirely distinct from the body, and is even easier to know than it, and even if the latter were not at all, the soul would not cease to be all that which it is. . . . And having noticed that there is nothing at all in this—*I think, therefore I am*—that would assure me that I am speaking the truth except that I see very clearly that, in order to think, it is necessary to be: I judged that I could take for a general rule that the things that we conceive very clearly and very distinctly are all true, but that there is only some difficulty in correctly recognizing which are the things that we conceive distinctly.

Following this, and reflecting upon the fact that I doubted, and that therefore, my being was not totally perfect, for I clearly saw that it is a greater perfection to know than to doubt, I decided to search for the source from which I had learned to think of something more perfect than I was, and I knew evidently that this had to be from some nature that were, in effect, more perfect.

[Descartes notes that things like heat and light possessed nothing in the conceptions he had of them that suggested they were more perfect than himself.]

But the same could not hold for the idea of a being more perfect than I am, for to obtain it from nothing was something manifestly impossible . . . it remained that this idea had been posited in me by a nature that truly was more perfect than I was, and that even possessed in itself all the perfections of which I could have any idea, that is to say, to express myself in one word, that were God. . . . I saw that doubt, inconstancy, sadness and similar things could not be there, seeing that I myself would have been quite happy to be exempt from them. . . .

After this I went in search of other truths, and having set before myself the object of the geometers . . . a space indefinitely extended in length, breadth and height or depth, divisible . . . I also took note that there was nothing at all in these demonstrations that were to assure me of the existence of their object. For I saw very well, for example, that supposing a triangle, it is necessary that its three angles were equal to two right ones, but I did not see anything, for all this, that assures me that there were any triangle in the world . . . the sense of sight assures us no less of the truth of its objects than do the senses of smell or hearing, whereas neither our imagination nor our senses could ever assure us of anything if our understanding did not intervene. . . . From whence does one know that the thoughts that occur in dreams are any more false than the others, seeing that they are often not less vivid?. . . Even that which I have already taken for a rule, namely, that the things that we conceive very clearly and very distinctly are all true, is assured only for the reasons that God is or exists, that he is a perfect being, and that all that which is in us comes from him. From whence it follows that our ideas or notions, being real things, and coming from God, in all that in which they are clear and distinct, cannot, in this, be anything but true. . . . All that is real and true in us comes from a perfect and infinite being, however clear and distinct our ideas were, we would not have any other reason to assure us that they had the perfection of being true . . . after the knowledge of God and of the soul has thus rendered us certain of this rule, it is very easy to know that the reveries that we have while being asleep ought in no way to make us doubt the truth of the thoughts that we have while being awake. . . . Finally whether we be awake or asleep, we ought never to let ourselves be persuaded except by the evidence of our reason. . . . All our ideas or notions must have some foundation in truth; for it would not be possible that God, who is totally perfect and totally truthful, would have posited them in us without that.

Part Five

I would here willingly have proceeded to show the whole chain of truths, which I deduced from these primary ones. But . . . it would be necessary now to speak about many questions that are in a state of controversy among the learned. I do not wish to quarrel . . . and would say only generally what these questions are. . . . I have recently . . . demonstrated the existence of God and the soul, and to accept as true nothing that did not appear to me more clear and certain than the demonstrations of the geometers had formerly appeared. . . . I have also observed certain laws established in nature by God . . . [and] it appears to me that I have discovered many truths more useful and more important than all I had before learned, or even had expected to learn.

But because I have tried to explain the principal ones of these truths in a treatise that certain considerations prevented me from publishing, I could not better make them known than by summarily saying here what it contains. . . . Being afraid of not being able to put into my discourse all that which I had in my thought, I undertook merely to give in it quite an ample exposition of that which I conceived with respect to light . . . then to add something about the sun and the fixed stars, because light proceeds almost totally from them, something about the heavens, because they transmit light, about the planets, the

comets and the earth, because they cause light to reflect, and in particular about all terrestrial bodies, because they are either colored, or
transparent, or luminous, and finally about man, because he is the
observer thereof. . . .

In order to show how I there handled this matter, I mean here to
give the explication of the motion of the heart and arteries, which as
the first and most general motion observed in animals, will afford the
means of readily determining what should be thought of all the rest.
And so that there may be less difficulty in understanding what I am
about to say on this subject, I advised those who are not versed in
anatomy before they commence the perusal of these observations, to
take the trouble of getting dissected in their presence the heart of
some large animal possessed of lung (for this is throughout sufficiently like the human), and to have shown to them its two ventricles
or cavities. . . .

*[Descartes goes on to describe the veins and arteries, the ventricles of the
heart, the way the blood flows through the heart, etc.]*

But least those who are ignorant of the force of mathematical
demonstrations, and who are not accustomed to distinguish true reasons from mere verisimilitudes, should venture without examination,
to deny what has been said, I wish it to be considered that the motion
which I have now explained follows as necessarily from the very
arrangement of the parts, which may be observed in the heart by the
eye alone, and from the heat which may be felt with the fingers, and
from the nature of the blood as learned from experience, as does the
motion of a clock from the power, the situation, and shape of its coun-
terweights and wheels. . . .

*[Descartes then discusses the work of Harvey and his discovery of the cir-
culation of the blood. Having used the analogy to the clock, he then carefully explains the difference between men and brutes and between living
matter and machines.]*

I have thus described the rational soul, and shown that in no way
can it be derived from the power of matter, as can the other things of
which I have spoken, but it must be expressly created; it does not suffice that it be lodged in the human body as a pilot in his ship, unless
perhaps to move its members, but rather the soul must be more
closely joined and united with the body in order to have sensations

and appetites similar to ours, and thus constitute a real man. As for the rest, I have here elaborated a little on the subject of the soul, because it is of the greatest importance; for, after the error of those who would deny God, which I think I have sufficiently refuted above, there is none at all more powerful in leading feeble minds astray from the straight path of virtue than the supposition that the soul of the brutes is of the same nature with our own. . . .

Part Six

[Descartes opens Part Six by saying that three years have passed and that in that time he learned of the condemnation of Galileo by the Roman Catholic Church. Of course, he never uses those words, referring rather only to men of authority "to whom I defer" and stating that until they acted he had never thought there was anything wrong with the views (of Galileo) that have been condemned, that is, with the assumption that the earth moved around the sun. For this reason, he says he put off publishing a longer treatise, what became his Principia *of 1644 and then his treatise on man published after his death. Yet clearly he wants the world to know his thinking about nature and his method.]*

But as soon as I had acquired some general notions respecting physics, and beginning to make trial of them in various particular difficulties, I had noticed whereto they can lead, and how much they differ from the principles that one has used until the present. I believed that I could not keep them concealed without sinning seriously against the rule that requires us as much as possible to strive for the common good of all men. For these notions have shown me that it is possible to arrive at knowledge that is very useful for living, and that in place of that speculative philosophy that is taught in the schools [i.e., Scholasticism], one can find a practical philosophy, by means of which, knowing the force and action of fire, water, air, the stars, the heavens, and all the other bodies that surround us, as distinctly as we know the various crafts of artisans, we might in the same fashion be able to use them for all uses that are appropriate, and thus to render ourselves the masters and possessors of nature. . . . I believe that it is in medicine that one ought to be searching for it . . . the science of medicine, as it now exists, contains few things of which the utility be so remarkable. . . . Now having the intention of spending my whole life in the search for a science so necessary, and having found a path that seems to me such that, by following it, one ought infallibly to find this science, if it were not that one be hindered therefrom either by the brevity of life or by the lack of observations. I judge that there was hardly any better remedy against these two obstacles than to communicate faithfully to the public all the little that I had found, and to urge the good minds to try to advance further by contributing, each according to his inclination and his ability. . . .

The order to which I have held in this has been the following: First, I have tried to find in general the principles or first causes of all that is or can be in the world, without taking into consideration this and anything but God alone, who has created it, and without drawing them from elsewhere than from the germs of truths existing naturally in our minds. After that, I have examined what are the first and most ordinary effects that can be deduced from these causes. . . . I have found the heavens, the stars, an earth, and even, on the earth, water, air, fire, minerals and some other such things that are the most common of all and the simplest, and as a consequence, the easiest to know. . . .

It is also necessary that I admit that the power of nature is so ample and so vast, and that these principles are so simple and so general, that I notice hardly any particular effect of which I would not at once know that it can be deduced from the principles in many different ways, and that ordinarily my greatest difficulty is to find out in which one of these ways it depends on them.

[Descartes then calls upon all "who are virtuous in fact" to assist him. After a somewhat convoluted explanation for why he has refrained from publishing the work that he really wanted everyone to read, Descartes continues his modestly phrased plea for the advancement of learning.]

I would very much like everyone to know that what little I have learned until now is almost nothing in comparison with that of which I am ignorant and which I am not despairing of being able to learn. . . . To try to vanquish all the difficulties and the errors that prevent us from arriving at the knowledge of the truth is truly to engage in battles. . . . I have already found some truths in the sciences. . . . I can only say that these are things resulting from and depending on five or six principal difficulties that I have surmounted and that I count as so many battles in which I have had fortune on my side. . . . I recognize that I am extremely liable to err, and that I almost never rely on the first thoughts that come to me, the experience that I have of the objections that one can make against me still prevents me from expecting any profit from them: for I have often been tested by the judgments both of those whom I take to be friends and of some others whom I knew their malice and envy would try hard enough to discover that which affection would find from my friends.... And I have never observed that by means of the disputatious practices in the schools anyone has discovered any truth of which one had previously been ignorant, for which each one tries to conquer the other, one expends one's time in trying to seem correct than at weighing the reasons for the one side and for the other, and those who have long been good lawyers are not by the same token later better judges....

I am sure that the most passionate of those who now follow Aristotle would believe themselves fortunate if they did have as much knowledge of nature as he has had of it, even if it were on the condition that they should never have any more thereof. They are like ivy, which tends never to climb higher than the trees that support it, and which often even descends again after it reached their tops, for it seems to me also that these people are descending again, that is to say, they are rendering themselves in some fashion less knowledgeable than if they abstained from studying; not content with knowing all that which is intelligently explained in their author, they want besides this, to find there the solutions to many difficulties about which he says nothing and about which he has perhaps never thought. Still, their manner of philosophizing is very convenient for those who have only very mediocre minds....

And if I am writing in French, which is the language of my country and not in Latin, the language of my teachers, it is because I am hoping that those who make use only of their totally pure natural reason will better judge my opinions than those who believe only in the ancient books....

7

ROBERT BOYLE

New Experiments Physico-Mechanical

1660

In the middle of political revolution and upheaval in England, Robert Boyle (1627–1691) brought the new science to a higher level. Boyle perfected modern experimental techniques by insisting on replication and by describing his interventions into nature in such minute detail that they could be tested. He also took a posture of caution and invented a scientific style that was skeptical and tentative. As one of the founders of London's Royal Society, he was also a key player in the social organization of the new science. In this excerpt, Boyle ties his central assumptions to experimental protocol. As he has established that the air is an entity, he turns to atomism "a heap of little bodies, lying one upon another" to explain its expansion or contraction. Boyle called his atomism "corpuscularianism" because he did not like the association of ancient atomism with atheism. At its essence, Boyle's philosophy of nature relied on actual contact between the minute particles that made up all bodies and on empirical, verifiable work. He saw himself as both a Baconian and a Cartesian, and he labored all his life to defeat Scholasticism. Unlike Descartes, Boyle sought not to make bold generalizations but to carefully amass information, replicate it, and offer it to the world as a tentative conclusion.

[Boyle begins by describing the many trials and errors he undertook to make his air pump.]

And after an unsuccessful trial or two of ways proposed by others, the . . . person fitted me with a pump . . . and to supply the second defect, it was considered that it would not perhaps prove impossible to leave in the glass to be emptied a hole large enough to put in a man's arm clothed, and, consequently, other bodies . . . to give your Lordship

---

From Robert Boyle, *New Experiments Physico-Mechanical* (Oxford: H. Hall, 1660).

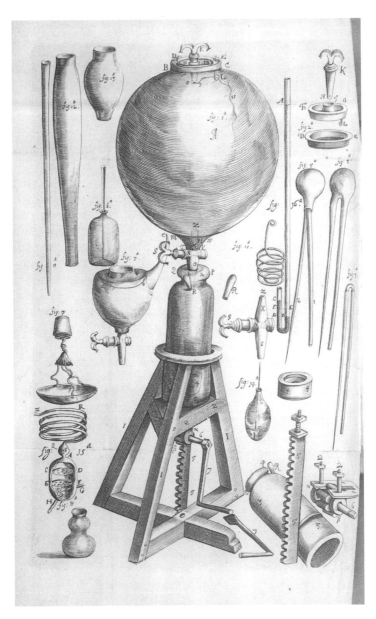

Figure 9. *Robert Boyle's Air Pump, 1660.*

Boyle's air pump was an unprecedented invention, an example of "big science" in its time.

This item is reproduced by permission of The Huntington Library, San Marino, California.

then . . . some account of the engine itself. It consists of two principal parts: a glass vessel and a pump to draw the air out of it. . . .

The undermost remaining part consists of a frame, and of a sucking pump, or as we formerly called it, an air pump, supported by it: The frame is of wood, small, but very strong, consisting of three legs (I I I)[1] so placed, that one side of it may stand perpendicular, that the free motion of the hand may not be hindered. . . .

The pump consists of four parts, a hollow cylinder, a sucker, a handle to move that sucker, and a valve. . . .

All things being thus fitted, and the lower shank (O)[2] of the stop-cock being put into the upper orifice of the cylinder (&), into which it was exactly ground, the experimenter is first, by turning the handle, to force the sucker to the top of the cylinder, that there may be no air left in the upper part of it. Then shutting the valve with the plug, and turning the other way, he is to draw down the sucker to the bottom of the cylinder, by which motion of the sucker, the air that was formerly in the cylinder being thrust out, and none being permitted to succeed in its room, 'tis manifest that the cavity of the cylinder must be empty in reference to the air. So that if thereupon the key of the stop-cock be so turned, as that through the perforation of it, a free passage be opened between the cylinder and the receiver part of the air formerly contained in the receiver will nimbly descend into the cylinder. And this air, being by the turning back of the key hindered from the returning into the receiver, may, by the opening of the valve, and forcing up of the sucker to the top of the cylinder again, be driven out into the open air. And thus by the repetition of the motion of the sucker upward and downward, and by opportunely turning the key, and stopping the valve, as occasion requires, more or less air may be sucked out of the receiver, according to the exigency of the experiment, and the intention of him that makes it.

Your Lordship will, perhaps, think that I have been unnecessarily prolix[3] in this first part of my discourse. But if you had seen how many unexpected difficulties we found to keep out the external air, even for a little while, when some considerable part of the internal had been sucked out, you would peradventure allow that I might have set down

---

[1]The letters refer to the labeling of items found in Figure 9.
[2]See Figure 9 for O, directly below the large round glass chamber, A.
[3]Boyle is notoriously prolix, i.e., wordy.

more circumstances than I have, without setting down any whose knowledge he that shall try the experiment may not have need of. Which is so true, that, before we proceed any further, I cannot think it unseasonable to advertise Your Lordship, that there are two chief sorts of experiments which we designed in our engine to make trial of: the one, such as may be quickly dispatched, and therefore may be tried in our engine, though it leak a little; because the air may be faster drawn out, by nimbly plying the pump, then it can get in at undiscerned leaks; I say at undiscerned leaks, because such as are big enough to be discovered can scarce be uneasy to be stopped. The other sort of experiments consists of those that require not only that the internal air be drawn out of the receiver, but that it be likewise for a long time kept out of it. Such are the preservation of animal and other bodies therein, the germination and growth of vegetables, and other trials of several sorts, which it is apparent cannot be well made unless the external air can, for a competent while, be excluded: Since even at a very small leak there may enough get in, to make the vacuum soon lose that name; by which I here declare once for all, that I understand not a space wherein there is no body at all, but such as is either altogether, or almost totally void of air. . . .

To proceed now to the phenomena, exhibited to us by the engine above described; I hold it not unfit to begin with what does constantly and regularly offer itself to our observation, as depending upon the fabric of the engine itself, and not upon the nature of this or that particular experiment which 'tis employed to try.

First, then upon the drawing down of the sucker (the valve being shut), the cylindrical space, deserted by the sucker, is left devoid of air, and therefore, upon the turning of the key, the air contained in the receiver rushes into the emptied cylinder, till the air in both those vessels be brought to about an equal measure of dilatation. And therefore, upon shutting the receiver by returning the key, if you open the valve, and force up the sucker again, you will find that after this first exsuction you will drive out almost a whole cylinder full of air. But at the following exsuctions, you will draw less and less of air out of the receiver into the cylinder because that there will still remain less and less air in the receiver itself, and consequently, the particles of the remaining air, having more room to extend themselves in, will less press out one another. This you will easily perceive by finding that you still force less and less air out of the cylinder, so that when the receiver is almost exhausted, you may force up the sucker almost to the top of the cylinder before you will need to unstop the valve to let out any air: And if at such time, the valve being shut, you let go the handle of the pump, you will find the sucker forcibly carried up to the top of the cylinder, by the protrusion of the external air, which, being much less rarefied than that within the cylinder, must have a more forcible pressure upon the sucker than the internal is able to resist: And by this means you may know how far you have emptied the receiver. And to this we may add, on this occasion, that constantly upon the turning of the key to let out the air from the receiver, into the emptied cylinder, there is immediately produced a considerably brisk noise, especially while there is any plenty of air in the receiver.

For the more easy understanding of the experiments tryable by our engine, I thought it not superfluous, nor unseasonable in the recital of this first of them, to insinuate that notion by which it seems likely that most, if not all, of them will prove explicable. Your Lordship will easily suppose, that the notion I speak of is, that there is a spring, or elastical power in the air we live in. By which . . . spring of the air, that which I mean is this: that our air either consists of, or at least abounds with, parts of such a nature, that in case they be bent or compressed by the weight of the incumbent part of the atmosphere, or by any other body, they do endeavor, as much as in them lies, to free themselves from that pressure, by bearing against the contiguous bodies that keep them bent, and as soon as those bodies are removed or reduced to give them way, by presently unbending and stretching out themselves, either quite, or so far forth as the contiguous bodies that resist them will permit, and thereby expanding the whole parcel of air, these elastical bodies compose.

This notion may perhaps be somewhat further explained by conceiving the air near the earth to be such a heap of little bodies, lying one upon another, as may be resembled to a fleece of wool. For this (to omit other likenesses between them) consists of many slender and flexible hairs, each of which may indeed, like a little spring, be easily bent or rolled up, but will also, like a spring, be still endeavoring to stretch itself out again. For though both these hairs, and the aerial corpuscles to which we liken them, do easily yield to external pressures; yet each of them (by virtue of its structure) is endowed with a power or principle of self-dilatation, by virtue whereof, though the hairs may by a man's hand be bent and crowded closer together, and into a narrower room than suits best with the nature of the body: Yet while they compose an endeavor outward, whereby it continually thrusts against the hand that opposes its expansion. . . .

There is yet another way to explicate the spring of the air, namely, by supposing with that most ingenious gentleman, Monsieur Descartes, that the air is nothing but a congeries or heap of small and (for the most part) of flexible particles of several sizes, and of all kind of figures which are raised by heat (especially that of the sun) into that fluid and subtle ethereal body that surrounds the earth, and by the restless agitation of that celestial matter wherein those particles swim, are so whirled round, that each corpuscle endeavors to beat off all others from coming within the little sphere requisite to its motion about its own center; and (in case any, by intruding into that sphere shall oppose its free rotation) to expel or drive it away. So that according to this doctrine, it imports very little, whether the particles of the air have the structure requisite to springs, or be of any other form (how irregular soever) since their elastical power is not made to depend upon their shape or structure, and (as it were) brandishing motion, which they receive from the fluid ether that swiftly flows between them, and whirling about each of them (independently from the rest) not only keeps those slender aerial bodies separated and stretched out (at least, as far as the neighboring ones will permit) which otherwise, by reason of their flexibleness and weight, would flag or curl, but also makes them hit against, and knock away each other, and consequently require more room, than that which if they were compressed, they would take up. . . .

[Boyle then wishes to demonstrate the weight of the air particles by showing the effect they have on sound.]

Conceiving it then the best way to make our trial with such a notice as might not be loud enough to make it difficult to discern slighter variations in it, but rather might be, both lasting, that we might take notice by what degrees it decreased; and so small, that it could not grow much weaker without becoming imperceptible. We took a watch, whose case we opened, that the contained air might have free egress into that of the receiver. And this watch was suspended in the cavity of the vessel only by a pack-thread, as the unlikeliest thing to convey a sound to the top of the receiver. And then closing up the vessel with melted plaster, we listened near the sides of it, and plainly enough heard the noise made by the balance. Those also of us that watched for that circumstance observed that the noise seemed to come directly in a straight line from the watch unto the ear. And it was observable to this purpose, that we found a manifest disparity of noise, by holding our ears near the sides of the receiver, and near the cover of it: which difference seemed to proceed from that of the texture of the glass, from the structure of the cover (and of the cement) through which the sound was propagated from the watch to the ear.

[Boyle then pumped the air out of the glass receiver in which the watch hung.]

But let us prosecute our experiment. The pump after this being employed, it seemed that from time to time the sound grew fainter and fainter, so that when the receiver was emptied as much as it used to be for the foregoing experiments, neither we, nor some strangers that chanced to be then in the room, could, by applying our ears to the very sides, hear any noise from within, though we could easily perceive that by moving of the hand which marked the second minutes, and by that of the balance, that the watch neither stood still, nor remarkably varied from its wonted motion. And to satisfy ourselves further that it was indeed the absence of the air about the watch that hindered us from hearing it, we let in the external air at the stop-cock, and then though we turned the key and stopped the valve, yet we could plainly hear the noise made by the balance, though we held our ears sometimes at two-foot distance from the outside of the receiver. And this experiment being reiterated in another place, succeeded after the like manner, which seems to prove that whether or not the air be the only, it is at least the principal medium of sounds. And by the way it is very well worth noting that in a vessel so well closed as our receiver, so weak a pulse as that of the balance of a watch should propagate a motion to the ear in a physically straight line, notwithstanding the interposition of so close a body as glass, especially glass of such thickness as that of our receiver.

[Boyle has achieved a number of his goals with the watch experiment. In a fashion that could be replicated he has shown the power of the air to carry sound, and in emptying his receiver he has also demonstrated the existence of a vacuum, something the Aristotelians like Suarez denied could exist.]

8

ROBERT BOYLE

A Free-Enquiry into the Vulgarly
Received Notion of Nature
1686

In A Free-Enquiry into the Vulgarly Received Notion of Nature, *Boyle wrote that the Scholastic notion of form was "vulgar," as in commonplace and wrong. The investigation of nature, Boyle had come to believe, was a way toward godliness. The moderns had made progress precisely because they had seen that nature does not do things through abstract principles like "[nature] abhors a vacuum" but through law-like regularities that can be discovered only through experimentation. By the time Boyle wrote his* Free-Enquiry, *his natural philosophy had reached maturity. He knew what he believed and what he thought to be nonsense. With his characteristic long-windedness and indirection, he laid out his position.*

I have often wondered that in so inquisitive an age as this, among those many learned men that have with much freedom, as well as acuteness, written of the works of nature (as they call them) and some of them of the principles too, I have not met with any that has made it his business to write of nature herself. . . .

I judged it very well worth the while to make, with philosophical freedom, a serious enquiry into the vulgarly received notion of nature; . . . And because many atheists ascribe so much to nature, that they think it needless to have recourse to a deity, for the giving an account of the phenomena of the universe: And, on the other side, very many theists seem to think the commonly received notion of nature little less than necessary to the proof of the existence and providence of God; I, who differ from both these parties, and yet think every true theist, and much more every true Christian, ought to be much concerned for truths that have so powerful an influence on religion,

From Robert Boyle, *A Free-Enquiry into the Vulgarly Received Notion of Nature: Made in an Essay* (London: H. Clark for John Taylor, 1686).

thought myself, for its sake, obliged to consider this matter, both with the more attention and with regard to religion. . . .

[For Boyle, the study of nature had become an expression of Christian piety. Boyle then rested his case on the progress made by the moderns, more precisely in proving the existence of the vacuum.]

And you will make no great difficulty to believe me if you consider that while men allow themselves so general and easy a way of rendering accounts of things that are difficult, as to attribute them to nature, shame will not reduce them to a more industrious scrutiny into the reasons of things, and curiosity itself will move them to it the more faintly, of which we have a clear and eminent example, in the ascension of water in pumps, and in other phenomena of that kind, whose true physical causes had never been found out, if the moderns had acquiesced, as their predecessors did, in that imaginary one, that the world was governed by a watchful being called nature and that she abhors a vacuum and consequently is still in a readiness to do irresistibly whatever is necessary to prevent it. Nor must we expect any great progress in the discovery of the true causes of nature effects while we are content to sit down with other than the particular and immediate ones.

9

ANTHONY VAN LEEUWENHOEK

Of the Formation of the Teeth in Several Animals; the Structure of the Human Teeth Explained . . .

1683

Anthony van Leeuwenhoek (1632–1723) (LAY-ven-hook is a close enough pronunciation) was a contemporary of the great painter Johannes Vermeer (1632–1675) and represents one of the most remarkable aspects of the movement toward a new science. A self-taught "amateur," Leeuwenhoek was conversant with the latest microscopic work being done in Europe and was not afraid to disagree with other experimenters when he thought they had made an error. Note in the excerpt from the letter that follows, Leeuwenhoek is assuming the uniformity of matter; thus, teeth from animals and humans may be compared. He also had a considerable interest in the causes of diseases and in assisting in the search for their cures.

Having taken great pains to investigate the formation of the elephant's tooth, and examined into the nature of it by every means I could devise, I found it to consist only of a collection of tubuli, or pipes, which are exceedingly small and all derive their origin from the inner part of the tooth, for I never could discover any of them lying longitudinally or lengthwise in it.

Upon examining that part of the tooth where the bony substance is but thin, which is where it is united to the head, I very plainly perceived that one end of these tubuli took its rise from the cavity within, and the other end extended to the circumference, which circumference or outside was composed of a kind of scaly particles laid one on another, and I considered with myself whether each series or layer of

From Anthony Leeuwenhoek, *The Select Works of Antony Van Leeuwenhoek, Containing His Microscopical Discoveries in Many of the Works of Nature*. Trans. from the Dutch and Latin editions published by the author, by Samuel Hoole, Vol. 1 (London: H. Fry, 1798), 114–15.

these scaly particles might not be the substance or thickness formed in the space of one year. . . .

I also examined the teeth taken from young hogs, and found them to be likewise formed of tubuli spreading from the cavity in the center, to the circumference.

After this, I was desirous of examining the structure of the human teeth, and having for that purpose procured a number of the large ones, called the grinders, I found them to be formed exactly in the manner before described, namely, of tubuli or little bony pipes, closely joined together, arising at the cavity in the middle of the tooth, and ending at the circumference or outside. And in order to explain this formation to the reader as clearly as possible, I caused the following drawings to be made. . . .

I cut away almost the half, not to discover the cavity therein, which is well known to most persons, but only to show the manner how the tubuli, of which the bony part is composed, take their rise from the cavity in the center, and terminate at the circumference. But it must be understood, that these tubuli are by no means of the size represented by the lines in this figure, the same only denoting the order in which they lie, for the tubuli themselves are exceedingly small, and cannot be well discerned without the help of the very best microscopes.

In the same figure . . . is represented another tooth which is filed down from the upper part of it as far as the before-mentioned cavity in order to show how the tubuli do here also spread themselves round about from the center. All the extremities of the tubuli which lie near the outside of the tooth (as far as they are above the gums, and exposed to the air) are extremely hard, being as it were the solid case or covering of the tooth, and if we examine the surface of this case or covering attentively, we shall find one tooth to have forty, another perhaps fifty circles on it, like wrinkles or gatherings, which in some places run in a curved or wavy direction, . . . where a drawing is given of this outside shell, with some of the circles marked thereon, and I imagine that the circles which thus appear like wrinkles proceed from hence, that they are the places where the tooth, while growing, is from time to time protruded or thrust out from the gum.

In the teeth shed by children, and likewise in those of many young animals, I have observed that the ends of their roots are entirely open or hollow, and in like manner I imagine that the roots of the molar teeth or grinders which I have been just describing are at first formed in the same manner, but that in process of time they become ossified or converted into a bony substance of a spongy nature, through which many vessels pass, conveying blood and nutritive juices into the cavity of the tooth, and I also conceive that this cavity is filled with nerves and vessels spreading themselves into so many branches that every one of the bony tubuli is thereby increased during the time of its growth, and afterward (while the tooth continues sound) nourished and supported. I also conjecture that these small vessels thus nourishing and supporting the bony tubuli do not end at the surface of the tooth (I mean, in that part of it which is within the gum) but that the aliment or nutritive substance has a continued course through these vessels, and that the ends of the bony tubuli are again converted into soft or pliable vessels, spreading through the gum, and that those vessels are what principally keep the tooth fixed in its place. . . .

10

ISAAC NEWTON

Letter to Philosophical Transactions
of the Royal Society

1672

Isaac Newton's (1643–1727) achievements were so important that they altered the Western understanding of nature profoundly. It became possible, indeed essential, to imagine nature as bounded by laws that are knowable through experimentation and mathematical explication. Newton came upon the outline of the law of universal gravitation, as well as a new understanding of the nature of light in one year—1666. Only gradually did he publish these insights. First he wrote to the Royal Society in 1672 and that letter is here printed in part. From his relative obscurity as a Cambridge professor, Newton writes with a complete mastery of experimental technique and with the ability to draw universally applicable conclusions, and in the process undo what had been the commonplace view of light, that it was uniform and indivisible.

From *Philosophical Transactions of the Royal Society* 80 (1672): 3075.

SIR,

To perform my late promise to you, I shall without further ceremony acquaint you, that in the beginning of the year 1666 (at which time I applied myself to the grinding of optic glasses of other figures than spherical) I procured me a triangular glass-prism, to try therewith the celebrated phenomena of colors. And in order thereto having darkened my chamber, and made a small hole in my window-shuts, to let in a convenient quantity of the sun's light, I placed my prism at his entrance, that it might be thereby refracted to the opposite wall. It was at first a very pleasing divertisement, to view the vivid and intense colors produced thereby, but after a while applying myself to consider them more circumspectly, I became surprised to see them in an *oblong* form, which, according to the received laws of refraction, I expected should have been *circular*.

They were terminated at the sides with straight lines, but at the ends the decay of light was so gradual that it was difficult to determine justly what was their figure, yet they seemed *semicircular*.

Comparing the length of this colored spectrum with its breadth, I found it about five times greater, a disproportion so extravagant that it excited me to a more than ordinary curiosity of examining from whence it might proceed. I could scarce think, that the various thickness of the glass, or the termination with shadow or darkness, could have any influence on light to produce such an effect, yet I thought it not amiss, first to examine those circumstances, and so tried, what would happen by transmitting light through parts of the glass of diverse thicknesses, or through holes in the window of diverse bignesses, or by letting the prism without so that the light might pass through it and be refracted before it was terminated by the hole. But I found none of those circumstances material. The fashion of the colors was in all these cases the same.

Then I suspected, whether by any unevenness in the glass, or other contingent irregularity, these colors might be thus dilated. And to try this, I took another prism like the former and so placed it that the light, passing through them both, might be refracted contrary ways, and so by the latter returned into that course, from which the former had diverted it. For, by this means I thought, the regular effects of the first prism would be destroyed be the second prism, but the irregular ones more augmented by the multiplicity of refractions. The event was that the light, which by the first prism was diffused into an *oblong* form, was by the second reduced into an *orbicular* one with as much regularity as when it did not at all pass through them. So that, what ever was the cause of that length, 'twas not any contingent irregularity.

I then proceeded to examine more critically what might be effected by the difference of the incidence of rays coming from diverse parts of the sun, and to that end measured the several lines and angles belonging to the image. Its distance from the hole or prism was 22 foot, its utmost length $13\frac{1}{4}$ inches, its breadth $2\frac{5}{8}$, the diameter of the hole $\frac{1}{4}$ of an inch the angle, with the rays, tending toward the middle of the image, made with those lines, in which they would have proceeded without refraction, was 44 deg. 56'. And the vertical angle of the prism, 63 deg. 12'. Also the refractions on both sides [of] the prism, that is, of the incident and emergent rays, were as near as I could make them, equal, and consequently about 54 deg. 4'. And the rays fell perpendicularly upon the wall. Now subducting the diameter of the hole from the length and breadth of the image, there remains 13 inches the length, and $2\frac{3}{8}$ the breadth, comprehended by those rays, which passed through the center of the said hole, and consequently the angle of the hole, which that breadth subtended, was about 31', answerable to the sun's diameter, but the angle, which its length subtended, was more than five such diameters, namely 2 deg. 49'.

Having made these observations, I first computed from them the refractive power of that glass, and found it measured by the ratio of the sines, 20 to 31. And then, by that ratio, I computed the refractions of two rays flowing from opposite parts of the sun's discus, so as to differ 31' in their obliquity of incidence, and found that the emergent rays should have comprehended an angle of about 31', as they did, before they were incident. . . .

The gradual removal of these suspicions at length led me to the *Experimentum Crucis*,[1] which was this: I took two boards, and placed one of them close behind the prism at the window, so that the light might pass through a small hole made in it for the purpose, and fall on the other board, which I placed at about 12 feet distance, having first made a small hole in it also for some of that incident light to pass through. Then I placed another prism behind this second board so that the light, trajected through both the boards, might pass through that also and be again refracted before it arrived at the wall. This done, I took the first prism in my hand and turned it to and fro slowly

---

[1] Crucial experiment.

about its axis, so much as to make the several parts of the image, cast on the second board, successively pass through the hole in it, that I might observe to what places on the wall the second prism would refract them.

And I saw by the variation of those places that the light, tending to that end of the image towards which the refraction of the first prism was made, did in the second prism suffer a refraction considerably greater than the light tending to the other end. And so the true cause of the length of that image was detected to be no other than that light consists of rays differently refrangible, which, without any respect to a difference in their incidence, were, according to their degrees of refrangibility, transmitted towards diverse parts of the wall. . . .

The doctrine you will find comprehended and illustrated in the following propositions.

1. As the rays of light differ in degrees of refrangibility, so they also differ in their disposition to exhibit this or that particular color. Colors are not qualifications of light, derived from refractions, or reflections of natural bodies (as 'tis generally believed) but original and connate properties, which in diverse rays are diverse. Some rays are disposed to exhibit a red color and no other; some a yellow and no other, some a green and no other, and so of the rest. Nor are there only rays proper and particular to the more eminent colors, but even to all their intermediate gradations.

2. To the same degree of refrangibility ever belongs the same color, and to the same color ever belongs the same degree of refrangibility. The least refrangible rays are all disposed to exhibit a red color, and contrarily those rays which are disposed to exhibit a red color are all the least refrangible. So the most refrangible rays are all disposed to exhibit a deep violet color and contrarily those which are apt to exhibit such a violet color are all the most refrangible. And so to all the intermediate colors in a continued series belong intermediate degrees of refrangibility. And this analogy between colors, and refrangibility, is very precise and strict; the rays always either exactly agreeing in both, or proportionally disagreeing in both.

3. The species of color and degree of refrangibility proper to any particular sort of rays is not mutable by refraction, nor by reflection from natural bodies, nor by any other cause that I could yet observe. . . .

11

ISAAC NEWTON

Selections from Principia

1687

The excerpt that follows, from the preface and text of Newton's master-work, Principia, *defines it as a work in mechanics, setting forth the law of universal gravitation in terms that any educated person of the age could understand. The* Principia *did nothing less, as Newton claimed, than as it says, "derive the forces of gravity by which bodies tend to the sun and the individual planets. Then from the forces, using propositions that are also mathematical, we deduce the motions of the planets, of comets, of the moon, and of the sea." No work in science had ever before delivered so much knowledge about the physical world. In the late eighteenth century when the French were reforming their scientific education to give it more of a focus toward application, they adopted a French translation of a Newtonian textbook by Desaguliers, one of Newton's friends and an early explicator of his science.*

Newton's Preface to the Reader

The ancients, as Pappus [d. 350 CE] wrote, made mechanics of the highest value in the investigation of natural matters, and more recent writers, having dismissed substantial forms and occult qualities, have made an approach to referring the phenomena of nature back to mathematical laws. It has accordingly seemed fitting in this treatise to develop mathematics insofar as it looks to philosophy. Now the ancients established two branches of mechanics: rational, which proceeds accurately by demonstrations; and practical. To practical mechanics all the manual arts look, and from here its name "mechanica" is borrowed. But since artisans are accustomed to work with little accuracy, it happens that mechanics as a whole is so distinguished from geometry, that whatever is accurate is referred to geometry, and

From Dana Densmore, ed., *Selections from Newton's* Principia (Santa Fe, N.M.: Green Lion Press, 2004), 3, and Isaac Newton, *Principia* (London: Joseph Streater for the Royal Society, 1687).

whatever is less accurate, to mechanics. The errors, however, belong
to the artisan, not the art. One who works less accurately is a more
imperfect mechanic, and if any could work with perfect accuracy, this
would be the most perfect mechanic of all. For the drawing of both
straight lines and circles, upon which geometry is founded, belongs to
mechanics. Geometry does not teach how to draw these lines, but
requires that they be drawn. For it requires that the beginner learn to
draw them accurately before crossing the threshold of geometry, and
then teaches how problems are solved by these operations. To draw
straight lines and circles are problems, but not geometrical problems.
The solution of these is required of mechanics, and once the solutions
are found, their use is taught in geometry. And it is the glory of geometry that so much is accomplished with so few principles that are
obtained elsewhere. Thus geometry is founded upon mechanical pro-
cedure, and is nothing else but that part of universal mechanics that
accurately sets forth and demonstrates the art of measuring. Further,
since the manual arts are chiefly concerned with making bodies move,
it happens that geometry is commonly related to magnitude, and
mechanics to motion. In this sense, rational mechanics will be the science of the motions that result from any forces whatever, and of the
forces that are required for any motions whatever, accurately set forth
and demonstrated. This part of mechanics was developed into five
powers by the ancients, looking to the manual arts, since they considered gravity (which is not a manual power) not otherwise than in the
weights that were to be moved by those powers. We, however, are
interested, not in the arts, but in philosophy, and write of powers that
are not manual but natural, treating mainly those matters pertaining to
gravity, levity, elastic force, the resistance of fluids, and forces of this
kind, whether attractive or impulsive. And on that account we present
these [writings] of ours as the mathematical principles of philosophy.
For the whole difficulty of philosophy appears to turn upon this: that
from the phenomena of motion we may investigate the forces of
nature, and then from these forces we may demonstrate the rest of the
phenomena. And to this end are aimed the general propositions to
which we have given careful study in the first and second books.[1] In
the third book, on the other hand, we present an example of this pro-
cedure, in the unfolding of the system of the world. For there, from
the celestial phenomena, using the propositions demonstrated mathe-

[1]The *Principia* was divided into three books or parts.

matically in the preceding books, we derive the forces of gravity by which bodies tend to the sun and the individual planets. Then from the forces, using propositions that are also mathematical, we deduce the motions of the planets, of comets, of the moon, and of the sea. In just the same way it would be possible to derive the rest of the phenomena of nature from mechanical principles by the same manner of argument. For I am led by many reasons to strongly suspect that all of them can depend upon certain forces by which the particles of bodies, by causes not yet known, either are impelled toward each other mutually and cohere in regular shapes, or flee from one another and recede. These forces being unknown, philosophers have hitherto probed nature in vain. It is my hope, however, that the principles set forth here will shed some light either upon this manner of philosophizing, or upon some truer one. . . .

Definitions

DEFINITION I. THE QUANTITY OF MATTER IS THE MEASURE OF THE SAME, ARISING FROM ITS DENSITY AND BULK CONJUNCTLY.

Thus air of a double density, in a double space, is quadruple in quantity; in a triple space, sextuple in quantity. The same thing is to be understood of snow, and fine dust or powders that are condensed by compression or liquefaction, and of all bodies that are by any causes whatever differently condensed. I have no regard in this place to a medium, if any such there is, that freely pervades the interstices between the parts of bodies. It is this quantity that I mean hereafter everywhere under the name of body or mass. And the same is known by the weight of each body: For it is proportional to the weight, as I have found by experiments on pendulums, very accurately made, which shall be shown hereafter.

DEFINITION II. THE QUANTITY OF MOTION IS THE MEASURE OF THE SAME, ARISING FROM THE VELOCITY AND QUANTITY OF MATTER CONJUNCTLY.

The motion of the whole is the sum of the motions of all parts; and therefore in a body double in quantity, with equal velocity, the motion is double; with twice the velocity, it is quadruple.

DEFINITION III. THE *VIS INSITA*, OR INNATE FORCE OF MATTER, IS A POWER OF RESISTING, BY WHICH EVERY BODY, AS MUCH AS IN IT LIES, ENDEAVORS TO PERSEVERE IN ITS PRESENT STATE, WHETHER IT BE OF REST, OR OF MOVING UNIFORMLY FORWARD IN A RIGHT LINE. . . .

DEFINITION IV. AN IMPRESSED FORCE IS AN ACTION EXERTED UPON A
BODY IN ORDER TO CHANGE ITS STATE, EITHER OF REST OR OF MOVING
UNIFORMLY FORWARD IN A RIGHT LINE. . . .

DEFINITION V. A CENTRIPETAL FORCE IS THAT BY WHICH BODIES ARE
DRAWN OR IMPELLED OR ANY WAY TEND TOWARD A POINT AS TO A
CENTER.

Of this sort is gravity by which bodies tend to the center of the earth;
magnetism, by which iron tends to the lodestone; and that force, whatever it is, by which the planets are perpetually drawn aside from the
rectilinear motions, which otherwise they would pursue, and made to
revolve in curvilinear orbits. A stone, whirled about in a sling, endeavors to recede from the hand that turns it, and by that endeavor dis-
tends the sling, and that with so much the greater force, as it is
revolved with the greater velocity, and as soon as ever it is let go, flies
away. That force which opposes itself to this endeavor, and by which
the sling perpetually draws back the stone towards the hand, and
retains it in its orbit, because 'tis directed to the hand as the center of
the orbit, I call the centripetal force. And the same thing is to be
understood of all bodies, revolved in any orbits. They all endeavor to
recede from the centers of their orbits, and were it not for the opposition of a contrary force which restrains them to and detains them in
their orbits, which I therefore call centripetal, would fly off in right
lines, with a uniform motion. A projectile, if it was not for the force of
gravity, would not deviate towards the earth, but would go off from it
in a right line and that with a uniform motion, if the resistance of the
air was taken away. 'Tis by its gravity that it is drawn aside perpetually
from its rectilinear course and made to deviate towards the earth
more or less according to the force of its gravity and the velocity of its
motion. The less its gravity is for the quantity of its matter, or the
greater the velocity with which it is projected, the less will it deviate
from a rectilinear course and the farther it will go. If a leaden ball projected from the top of a mountain by the force of gunpowder with a
given velocity, and in a direction parallel to the horizon, is carried in a
curved line to the distance of two miles before it falls to the ground,
the same, if the resistance of the air was took away, with a double or
decuple[2] velocity, would fly twice or ten times as far. And by increasing the velocity, we may at pleasure increase the distance to which it

[2] Ten-fold.

might be projected, and diminish the curvature of the line, which it might describe, till at last it should fall at the distance of 10, 30, or 90 degrees, or even might go quite round the whole earth before it falls, or lastly, so that it might never fall to the earth, but go forward into the celestial spaces, and proceed in its motion *in infinitum*. And after the same manner, that a projectile, by the force of gravity, may be made to revolve in an orbit and go round the whole earth, the moon also, either by the force of gravity, if it is endued with gravity, or by any other force that impels it towards the earth, may be perpetually drawn aside towards the earth, out of the rectilinear way, which by its innate force it would pursue; and be made to revolve in the orbit which it now describes: nor could the moon without some such force be retained in its orbit. If this force was too small, it would not sufficiently turn the moon out of a rectilinear course. If it was too great, it would turn it too much, and draw down the moon from its orbit towards the earth. It is necessary that the force be of a just quantity, and it belongs to the mathematicians to find the force that may serve exactly to retain a body in a given orbit, with a given velocity, and vice versa, to determine the curvilinear way into which a body projected from a given place, with a given velocity, may be made to deviate from its natural rectilinear way, by means of a given force.

The quantity of any centripetal force may be considered as of three kinds: absolute, accelerative, and motive.

12

ISAAC NEWTON

Thirty-first Query to the Opticks

1718

Newton did not put all his optical theories together until 1704 when he published the Opticks. *Over several editions, he added queries — questions to be discussed by the scholarly community of natural philosophers. The thirty-first query (1718, second edition) is the most famous of these, and it set the agenda for the new science of chemistry and the study of electricity for decades to come. It presumes attractive forces at work throughout nature, and its structure is further presumed to be atomic.*

Have not the small particles of bodies certain powers, virtues, or forces by which they act at a distance, not only upon the rays of light for reflecting, refracting, and inflecting them, but also upon one another for producing a great part of the phenomena of nature? For it's well known that bodies act one upon another by the attractions of gravity, magnetism, and electricity, and these instances show the tenor and course of nature, and make it not improbable but that there may be more attractive powers than these. For nature is very consonant and conformable to herself. How these attractions may be performed, I do not here consider.[1] What I call attraction may be performed by impulse, or by some other means unknown to me. I use that word here to signify only in general any force by which bodies tend towards one another, whatsoever be the cause. For we must learn from the phenomena of nature what bodies attract one another, and what are the laws and properties of the attraction, before we inquire the cause by which the attraction is performed. The attractions of gravity, magnetism, and electricity reach to very sensible distances, and so have

---

[1]Newton consistently refused to say what gravity is. In private conversation he was known to say that it is the will of God operating in the universe.

From Isaac Newton, *Opticks* (London: W & J Innys, 1718), pp. 350–550.

been observed by vulgar[2] eyes, and there may be others which reach to so small distances as hitherto escape observation, and perhaps electrical attraction may reach to such small distances, even without being excited by friction. . . .

Or why does not salt of tartar draw more water out of the air than in a certain proportion to its quantity, but for want of an attractive force. . . .

When spirit of vitriol[3] poured upon common salt or saltpeter makes an ebullition with the salt, and unites with it, and in distillation the spirit of the common salt or saltpeter comes over much easier than it would do before, and the acid part of the spirit of vitriol stays behind, does not this argue that the fixed alcaly[4] of the salt attracts the acid spirit of the vitriol more strongly than its own spirit, and not being able to hold them both, lets go its own? And when oil of vitriol is drawn off from its weight of niter, and from both the ingredients a compound spirit of niter is distilled, and two parts of this spirit of niter are poured on one part of oil of cloves or caraway seeds, or of any ponderous oil of vegetable or animal substances, or oil of turpentine thickened with a little balsam of sulphur, and the liquors grow so very hot in mixing as presently to send up a burning flame, does not this very great and sudden heat argue that the two liquors mix with violence, and that their parts in mixing run towards one another with an accelerated motion, and clash with the greatest force? And is it not for the same reason that well rectified spirit of wine poured on the same compound spirit flashes, and that the *pulvis fulminans*, composed of sulphur, niter, and salt of tartar, goes off with a more sudden and violent explosion than gunpowder, the acid spirits of the sulphur and niter rushing towards one another, and towards the salt of tartar, with so great a violence, as by the shock to turn the whole at once into vapor and flame? Where the dissolution is slow, it makes a slow ebullition and a gentle heat, and where it is quicker, it makes a great ebullition with more heat, and where it is done at once, the ebullition is contracted into a sudden blast or violent explosion, with a heat equal to that of fire and flame. So when a drachm[5] of the above-mentioned compound spirit of niter was poured upon half a drachm of oil of caraway seeds *in vacuo*, the mixture immediately made a flash like

---

[2]Ordinary.
[3]Sulfuric acid.
[4]Alkaline of salt used as a solvent.
[5]Dram, a weight of about $\frac{1}{8}$ of an ounce; today it is $\frac{1}{16}$ of an ounce.

gunpowder and burst the exhausted receiver, which was a glass six inches wide and eight inches deep. And even the gross body of sulphur powdered, and with an equal weight of iron filings and a little water made into paste, acts upon the iron, and in five or six hours grows too hot to be touched, and emits a flame. And by these experiments compared with the great quantity of sulphur with which the earth abounds, and the warmth of the interior parts of the earth, and hot springs, and burning mountains, and with damps, mineral coruscations, earthquakes, hot suffocating exhalations, hurricanes, and spouts, we may learn that sulphurous steams abound in the bowels of the earth and ferment with minerals, and sometimes take fire with a sudden coruscation and explosion, and if pent up in subterraneous caverns, burst the caverns with a great shaking of the earth, as in springing of a mine. And then the vapor generated by the explosion, expiring through the pores of the earth, feels hot and suffocates, and makes tempests and hurricanes, and sometimes causes the land to slide, or the sea to boil, and carries up the water thereof in drops, which by their weight fall down again in spouts. Also some sulphurous steams, at all times when the earth is dry, ascending into the air, ferment there with nitrous acids, and sometimes taking fire cause lightning and thunder, and fiery meteors. For the air abounds with acid vapors fit to promote fermentations, as appears by the rusting of iron and copper in it, the kindling of fire by blowing, and the beating of the heart by means of respiration. Now the above-mentioned motions are so great and violent as to show that in fermentations the particles of bodies which almost rest are put into new motions by a very potent principle, which acts upon them only when they approach one another, and causes them to meet and clash with great violence, and grow hot with the motion, and dash one another into pieces, and vanish into air, and vapor, and flame. . . .

13

CHRISTIAAN HUYGENS

The Celestial Worlds Discovered

1698

Christiaan Huygens (1629–1695) came from an educated Dutch family and spent many years in Paris affiliated with the Academy of Science there. He perfected the pendulum clock and a version of the pocket watch, and he made brilliant astronomical observations, discovering the rings of Saturn among other heavenly objects (in the book presented here, Huygens refers to them quaintly as "the little gentlemen round Jupiter and Saturn").[1] In his boldest work, published after his death, Huygens considered the possibility of life on other planets. He did so at a time when such ideas were increasingly commonplace but also considered radical and dangerous. As the opening pages make clear, Huygens knew what controversy he would arouse. Indeed in 1600, Giordano Bruno (1548–1600) had been burned at the stake in Rome for ideas similar yet more extreme.[2]

In this excerpt, Huygens addresses the religious objections of his contemporaries who said that such new worlds and their inhabitants could not exist because the Bible makes no mention of them. Huygens saw speculations about life on other planets as a logical outgrowth of the work of Copernicus and Galileo.

A man that is of Copernicus's opinion, that this earth of ours is a planet, carried round and enlightened by the sun, like the rest of

---

[1]For a technical treatment of his science, see Joella G. Yoder, *Unrolling Time: Christiaan Huygens and the Mathematization of Nature* (Cambridge: Cambridge University Press, 1998, 2004). See also Lisa Jardine, *Going Dutch: How England Plundered Holland's Glory* (New York: HarperCollins, 2008), especially chap. 10 on the complexity of who has priority on perfecting the clocks.

[2]Steven J. Dick, *Plurality of Worlds: The Origins of the Extraterrestrial Life Debate from Democritus to Kant* (Cambridge: Cambridge University Press, 1982).

From Christianus Huygens, *New Conjectures Concerning the Planetary Worlds: Their Inhabitants and Productions* (London: T. Childe, 1698).

them, cannot but sometimes have a fancy that it's not improbable that the rest of the planets have their dress and furniture, nay and their inhabitants too as well as this earth of ours: especially if he considers the later discoveries made since Copernicus's time of the attendants of Jupiter and Saturn, and the champain and hilly countries in the moon,[3] which are an argument of a relation and kin between our earth and them, as well as proof of the truth of that system. This has often been our talk, I remember, good Brother, over a large telescope, when we have been viewing those bodies, a study that your continual business and absence have interrupted for this many years. But we were always apt to conclude that 'twas in vain to inquire after what nature had been pleased to do there, seeing there was no likelihood of ever coming to an end of the inquiry. Nor could I ever find that any philosophers, those bold heroes, either ancient or modern, ventured so far. At the very birth of astronomy, when the earth was first asserted to be spherical and to be surrounded with air, even then there were some men so bold as to affirm there were an innumerable company of worlds in the stars. But later authors such as Cardinal Cusanus, Brunus, Kepler (and if we may believe him, Tycho was of that opinion too)[4] have furnished the planets with inhabitants. . . . But a while ago thinking somewhat seriously of this matter (not that I count myself quicker sighted than those great men, but that I had the happiness to live after most of them) methoughts the inquiry was not so impracticable, nor the way so stopped up with difficulties, but that there was very good room left for probable conjectures. As they came into my head, I clapped them down into common places and shall now try to digest them in some tolerable method for your better conception of them, and add somewhat of the sun and fixed stars, and the extent of that universe of which our earth is but an inconsiderable point. I know you have such an esteem and reverence for anything that belongs to Heaven, that I persuade myself you will read what I have written without pain. . . . I could wish indeed that our world might not be my judges, but that I might choose my readers, men like you,[5] not ignorant in astronomy and true philosophy, for with such I might promise myself a favorable hearing and not need to make an apology for daring to vent anything new to the world. But because I am aware what other

[3]First discovered by Galileo.
[4]Nicolas of Cusa (1401–1464), Giordano Bruno, Johannes Kepler, and Tycho Brahe all thought about the possibility of planetary life.
[5]Addressed to his brother.

hands it's likely to fall into, and what a dreadful sentence I may expect from those whose ignorance or zeal is too great, it may be worth the while to guard myself beforehand against the assaults of those sort of people.

There's one sort who, knowing nothing of geometry or mathematics, will laugh at it as a whimsical and ridiculous undertaking. It's mere conjuration to them to talk of measuring the distance or magnitude of the stars. And for the motion of the earth, they count it, if not a false, at least a precarious opinion, and no wonder then if they take what's built upon such a slippery foundation for the dreams of a fanciful head and a distempered brain. What should we answer to these men, but that their ignorance is the cause of their dislike, and that if they had more sense they would have fewer scruples? But few people having had an opportunity of prosecuting these studies, either for want of parts, learning, or leisure, we cannot blame their ignorance, and if they resolve to find fault with us for spending time in such matters, because they do not understand the use of them, we must appeal to proper judges.

The other sort, when they hear us talk of new lands and animals endued with as much reason as themselves, will be ready to fly out into religious exclamations, that we set up our conjectures against the word of God and broach opinions directly opposite to Holy Writ. For we do not there read one word of the production of such creatures, no not so much as of their existence; nay rather we read quite the contrary. For that only mentions this earth with its animals and plants, and man the lord of them, but as for worlds in the sky, 'tis wholly silent. Either these men resolve not to understand, or they are very ignorant, for they have been answered so often that I am almost ashamed to repeat it: that it's evident God had no design to make a particular enumeration in the Holy Scriptures of all the works of his creation. When therefore it is plain that under the general name of stars or earth are comprehended all the heavenly bodies, even the little gentlemen round Jupiter and Saturn, why must all that multitude of beings which the almighty creator has been pleased to place upon them be excluded the privilege and not suffered to have a share in the expression? And these men themselves can't but know in what sense it is that all things are said to be made for the use of man, not certainly for us to stare or peep through a telescope at, for that's little better than nonsense. Since then the greatest part of God's creation, that innumerable multitude of stars, is placed out of the reach of any man's eye, and many of them, it's likely, of the best glasses, so that they don't seem to belong to us; is it such an unreasonable opinion, that there are some reasonable creatures who see and admire those glorious bodies at a nearer distance?

But perhaps they'll say it does not become us to be so curious and inquisitive in these things which the *supreme creator* seems to have kept for his own knowledge. For since he has not been pleased to make any farther discovery or revelation of them, it seems little better than presumption to make any inquiry into that which he has thought fit to hide. But these gentlemen must be told that they take too much upon themselves when they pretend to appoint how far and no farther men shall go in their searches, and to set bounds to other men's industry, just as if they had been of the privy council of heaven, as if they knew the marks that God has placed to knowledge, or as if men were able to pass those marks. If our forefathers had been at this rate scrupulous, we might have been ignorant still of the magnitude and figure of the earth, or of such a place as America. The moon might have shone with her own light for us all, and we might have stood up to the ears in water, like the Indians at every eclipse, and a hundred other things brought to light by the late discoveries in astronomy had still been unknown to us. For what can a man imagine more abstruse, or less likely to be known, than what is now as clear as the sun? That vigorous industry and that piercing wit were given men to make advances in the search of nature, and there's no reason to put any stop to such inquiries. I must acknowledge still that what I here intend to treat of is not of that nature as to admit of a certain knowledge; I can't pretend to assert anything as positively true (for that would be madness) but only to advance a probable guess, the truth of which everyone is at his own liberty to examine. If anyone therefore shall gravely tell me that I have spent my time idly in a vain and fruitless inquiry after what by my own acknowledgment I can never come to be sure of, the answer is that at this rate he would put down all natural philosophy as far as it concerns itself in searching into the nature of things. . . . For here we may mount from this dull earth, and viewing it from on high, consider whether nature has laid out all her cost and finery upon this small speck of dirt. So, like travelers into other distant countries, we shall be better able to judge of what's done at home, know how to make a true estimate of, and set its own value upon everything. We shall be less apt to admire what this world calls great, shall nobly despise those trifles the generality of men set their affections on, when we know that there are a multitude of such earths inhabited and adorned as well as our own. And we shall worship and reverence that God the maker of all these things; we shall admire and adore his providence and wonderful wisdom which is displayed and manifested all over the universe, to the confusion of those who would have the earth and all things formed by the shuffling concourse of atoms, or to be without beginning. . . . This must be our method in this treatise, wherein from the nature and circumstances of that planet which we see before our eyes, we may guess at those that are farther distant from us.

And, first, 'tis more than probable that the bodies of the planets are solid like that of our earth, and that they don't want what we call gravity, that virtue which like a lodestone attracts whatsoever is near the body to its center. And that they have such a quality, their very figure is a proof, for their roundness proceeds only from an equal pressure of all their parts tending to the same center. Nay more, we are so skillful nowadays as to be able to tell how much more or less the gravitation of Jupiter or Saturn is than here, of which discovery and its author you may read my *Essay of the Causes of Gravitation.*

But now to carry the search farther, let us see by what steps we must rise to the attaining some knowledge in the more private secrets concerning the state and furniture of these new earths. And, first, how likely is it that they may be stocked with plants and animals as well as we? I suppose nobody will deny but that there's somewhat more of contrivance, somewhat more of miracle in the production and growth of plants and animals than in lifeless heaps of inanimate bodies, be they never so much larger as mountains, rocks, or seas are. For the finger of God, and the wisdom of Divine Providence, is in them much more clearly manifested than in the other. One of Democritus's[6] or Cartes's[7] scholars may venture perhaps to give some tolerable explication of the appearances in heaven and earth, allow him but his atoms and motion, but when he comes to plants and animals, he'll find himself nonplussed, and give you no likely account of their production. For everything in them is so exactly adapted to some design, every part of them so fitted to its proper use, that they manifest an infinite wisdom, and exquisite knowledge in the laws of nature and geometry, as, to omit those wonders in generation, we shall by and by show, and make it an absurdity even to think of their being thus haply jumbled together by a chance motion of I don't know what little particles. Now should we allow the planets nothing but vast deserts, lifeless and inanimate stocks and stones, and deprive them of all those creatures that

---

[6]Democritus (ca. 460 BCE–ca. 370 BCE) was an ancient atomist.
[7]Descartes.

more plainly speak their divine architect, we should sink them below the earth in beauty and dignity, a thing that no reason will permit, as I said before. . . .

But still the main and most diverting point of the inquiry is behind, which is the placing some spectators in these new discoveries, to enjoy these creatures we have planted them with, and to admire their beauty and variety. And among all that have never so slightly meddled with these matters, I don't find any that have scrupled to allow them their inhabitants: not men perhaps like ours, but some creatures or other endued with reason. For all this furniture and beauty the planets are stocked with seem to have been made in vain, without any design or end, unless there were some in them that might at the same time enjoy the fruits and adore the wise creator of them. But this alone would be no prevailing argument with me to allow them such creatures. For what if we should say that God made them for no other design but that he himself might see (not as we do 'tis true, but that he that made the eye sees, who can doubt?) and delight himself in the contemplation of them? For was not man himself, and all that the whole world contains, made upon this very account? That which makes me of this opinion, that those worlds are not without such a creature endued with reason, is that otherwise our earth would have too much the advantage of them, in being the only part of the universe that could boast of such a creature so far above not only plants and trees, but all animals whatsoever: a creature that has a divine somewhat within him, that knows and understands and remembers such an innumerable number of things, that deliberates, weighs, and judges of the truth, a creature upon whose account, and for whose use, whatsoever the earth brings forth seems to be provided. For every thing here he converts to his own ends. . . .

Well, but allowing these planetarians some sort of reason, must it needs be the same with ours? Why truly I think 'tis, and must be so, whether we consider it as applied to justice and morality, or exercised in the principles and foundations of science. For reason with us is that which gives us a true sense of justice and honesty, praise, kindness, and gratitude: 'Tis that that teaches us to distinguish universally between good and bad, and renders us capable of knowledge and experience in it. And can there be anywhere a reason contrary to this? or can what we call just and generous in Jupiter or Mars be thought unjust villainy? This is not at all, I don't say probable, but possible. For the aim and design of the creator is every where the preservation and safety of his creatures. Now when such a reason as we are masters of is necessary for the preservation of life and promoting of society (a thing that they be not without, as we shall show) would it not be strange that the planetarians should have such a perverse sort of reason given them, as would necessarily destroy and confound what it was designed to maintain and defend? . . .

What is it then after all that sets human reason above all other and makes us preferable to the rest of the animal world? Nothing in my mind so much as the contemplation of the works of God, and the study of nature, and the improving those sciences which may bring us to some knowledge in their beauty and variety. For without knowledge what would be contemplation? And what difference is there between a man, who with a careless supine negligence views the beauty and use of the sun, and the fine golden furniture of the heaven, and one who with a learned niceness searches into their courses, who understands wherein the fixed stars, as they are called, differ from the planets, and what is the reason of the regular vicissitude of the seasons, who by sound reasoning can measure the magnitude and distance of the sun and planets? . . . If therefore the principle we before laid down be true, that the other planets are not inferior in dignity to ours, what follows but that they have creatures not to stare and wonder at the works of nature only, but who employ their reason in the examination and knowledge of them, and have made as great advances therein as we have? They do not only view the stars, but they improve the science of astronomy, nor is there anything can make us think this improbable, but that fond conceitedness of everything that we call our own, and that pride that is too natural to us to be easily laid down.

This supposition of their knowledge and use of astronomy in the planetary worlds will afford us many new conjectures about their manner of life and their state as to other things.

For, first: No observations of the stars that are necessary to the knowledge of their motions can be made without instruments, nor can these be made without metal, wood, or some such solid body. . . . Then the necessity in such observations of marking down the epochs or accounts of time, and of transmitting them to posterity, will force us to grant them the art of writing; I won't say the same with ours which is commonly used, but I dare affirm not more ingenious or easy. For how much more ready and expeditious is our way, than by that multitude of characters used in China, and how vastly preferable to knots tied in cords, or the pictures in use about the barbarous people of Mexico and Peru? There's no nation in the world but has some way or other of writing and marking down their thoughts: So that it's no wonder if the planetarians have been taught it by that great school-mistress necessity, and apply it to the study of astronomy and other sciences. . . .

But for all our large and liberal allowances to these gentlemen, they will still be behind-hand with us. For we have so certain a knowledge of the true system and frame of the universe; we have so admirable an invention of telescopes to help our failing eyesight in the view of the bigness and different forms of the planetary bodies, in the discovery of the mountains, and the shadows of them on the surface of the moon, in the bringing to light an innumerable multitude of stars other-wise invisible, that we must necessarily be far their masters in that knowledge. What must I do here? I could find in my heart (and I can see no reason why I may not, except it be to flatter and complement ourselves in being the only people that have the advantage of such excellent inventions) either to allow these planetary inhabitants such sharp eyes as not to need them, or else the use of glasses to help the deficiency of their sight. . . .

But somebody may perhaps object, and that not without reason at first sight, that the planetarians it's likely are destitute of all refined knowledge, just as the Americans were before they had commerce with the Europeans. For if one considers the ignorance of those nations, and of others in Asia and Africa equally barbarous, it will appear as if the main design of the creator in placing men upon the earth was that they might live, and, in a just sense of all the blessings and pleasure they enjoy, worship the fountain of their happiness, but that some bold fellows have leapt over the bounds of nature, and made searches into those forbidden depths only out of an affectation of knowing more than they were made for. There does not want an answer for these men. For God could not but foresee the advances men would make, in their inquiring into the affairs of heaven: that they would discover arts useful and advantageous to life: that they would cross the seas, and dig up the bowels of the earth. Nothing of all this could happen contrary to the mind and knowledge of the infi-nite author of all things. And if he foresaw these things would be, he so appointed and destined them to human kind. And the studies of arts and sciences cannot be said to be contrary to nature, since in the search thereof they are employed, especially if we consider the natural desire and love of knowledge rooted in all men. For it's impossible this should have been given them upon no design or account. But they will urge that if such a knowledge is natural, if we were born for it, why are there so very few, especially in astronomy, that prosecute these studies? For Europe is the only quarter of the earth in which there have been any advancements made in astronomy.

14

MARIA SIBYLLA MERIAN

Letter about Her Scientific Work
1702

Maria Sibylla Merian (1647–1717) was a German-born artist and naturalist. In this letter to a German physician, Merian describes her painstaking work with worms and caterpillars that she observed daily in the Dutch colony of Suriname. Her sense of wonder at nature is palpable as is the danger that the journey entailed. As a woman, Merian could make important contributions to early science but also be overlooked by the usual narratives of the period. She has received far more attention in art history than in the history of science. As this document makes clear, Merian had a deep desire to see her work published. She was looking for prepublication subscribers who would advance money and receive a discount when the plates were published. Merian might best be described as a scientific entrepreneur who financed her own research, kept in touch with others who might supply her with specimens, and thought it necessary for scientific observation to reach as wide an audience as possible.

Mr. Johan Georg Volkammer, Medicinal doctor in Nuremberg Monsieur!

As the gentleman has honored me with a letter of greeting, I can do no less than affirm my obligation herein and offer my service with all due respect in any way I can be of assistance to the gentlemen here in this country. First I should report to the gentleman that, having

Kurt Wettengl, ed., *Maria Sibylla Merian, 1647–1717: Artist and Naturalist* (Ostfildern-Kemnat, Germany: Verlad Gerd Hatje, 2003), 265–66.

returned from America,[1] I continued my work and am still doing it, bringing everything I sought and found in said America to parchment in its full perfection, which I hope to have finished if good health permits within two months. This consists of a collection of the worms and caterpillars I nourished daily with food, observing them until they achieved complete transformation, having previously painted and described the worms and caterpillars and the type and properties of their food while in that country. But everything I did not need to paint I have brought with me, such as the butterflies and beetles and everything I was able to preserve in brandy as well as everything I was able to dry. I am painting these things now, in the same manner as I did before in Germany, but am now putting everything on parchment on large folio sheets, the plants and animals in life size. Quite curious, as there are many wondrous, rare things in them that have never come to light before. And no one would so easily undertake such a hard and costly journey for such things. And the heat in this country is staggering, so that one can do no work at all without great difficulty, and I myself nearly paid for that with my death, which is why I could not stay there longer. And many were surprised that I survived, as most people die there because of the heat. Thus this work is not only rare now but will surely remain so.

I wish to have it printed for the benefit and pleasure of scholars and lovers of such things, so that they might see what wondrous plants and animals the Lord God has created in America, but as it will cost a lot of money to publish it, I shall be able to do so only if it can be financed in the manner of a subscription, as in the case of the Ambon work. It would have to contain 60 copper engravings at first, making it larger than the work in the Amsterdam Hortus Medicus, and it is then well subscribed or sold, so that I could recover my travel expenses in that way, another part could then be done, containing all kinds of other animals, such as snakes, crocodiles, iguanas and the like as well as East Indian fauna, for my youngest daughter's husband has since gone there as chief surgeon and will do his utmost to find as many things as possible. Therefore, I ask the gentleman to consider this matter together with other knowledgable scholars and to advise me as to how I could best accomplish this without loss and to the contentment of the gentlemen scholars and collectors. For if I were to sell the painted works, they would be worth the money and the expenses of

[1]Suriname.

the journey due to their great rarity, but then only one person would have them, and it will cost a great deal to publish it, as I have suggested above. But if a great number of collectors were to subscribe and pay in advance upon subscription, I would suffer no loss and could dare to undertake it.

I have also brought with me all of the animals comprised in this work, dried and well preserved in boxes, so that they can be seen by all.

I also currently still have jars with liquid containing one crocodile, many kinds of snakes and other animals, as well as about twenty round boxes of various butterflies, beetles, hummingbirds, lantern flies, referred to in the Indies as lute-players because of the sound they make, and other animals which are for sale. If the gentleman desires to have them, he need only so order. I also have people in America who catch such animals and send them for me to sell, and I also hope to receive things from the Spanish West Indies, as soon as the way has opened to allow ships to travel there. When that will happen only God knows.

As soon as I have obtained more such things I shall inform Mr. Schrey,[2] hoping I can provide it for the gentleman. With cordial greetings I remain the gentleman's

Devoted servant
Maria Sybilla Merian
please extend my
greetings to all mutual friends
who ask for me
Amsterdam, October 8th, 1702

[2] A mutual acquaintance.

MARIA SIBYLLA MERIAN

Butterfly, Hawk-moth, Caterpillar

1705

In this illustration, Merian mixed three different families as each—the butterfly, the moth, and the caterpillar—is not related to the other. She described in her text the history of her discoveries and the details of the family's breeding, but then she appears to have mixed up her specimens. This is not surprising given that she was working back home from notes that she had taken when in Suriname. The most important aspect of the watercolor painting, however, lies in its attempt to explain the secret of the butterfly's metallic luster. She examined the wing under a magnifying glass and discovered that it was made of overlapping layers, or scales, like tiles on a roof. Her brushstrokes sought to convey the layering.

The flower—a swallowtail—can be found throughout South America. The pomegranate, however, was not native to Suriname and was either brought there by travelers from the eastern Mediterranean or possibly sketched from observations Merian made in Europe. In her work, art and science merged to offer beauty as well as knowledge.

Philosophical Transactions of the Royal Society
1713–1714

The Philosophical Transactions of the Royal Society *was one of a number of publications that spread and heralded the new science. In this excerpt, the editor printed a notice from a German publication about a book in Latin that appeared in Padua (still a major medical university and center) about a contagious disease afflicting oxen and cattle. The communication was intended to reach as wide an audience as possible — anyone who could read Latin could read it in its entirety; if they preferred a summary, they could read this brief notice. Isaac Newton was president of the Royal Society when it published this piece. He came from a farm in Lincolnshire and would have known intimately how important the health of livestock could be. Part of the success and survival of entities like the Royal Society lay precisely in the willingness to survey all of nature and to strive for utility and application.*

It is now (at the publishing [of] the discourse) a year and [a] half, since a dreadful, unexpected and violent contagion has seized the black cattle, which, like an increasing fire, could neither be extinguished nor stopped by any human means.

This first began to be observed a little in *Agro Vincentino*, and soon discovered itself more openly in the country, spreading itself every way even to the very suburbs of Padua, with a cruel destruction of the cows and oxen. It has also been taken notice of in Germany in many places, nor has it been yet wholly conquered, *Publick News* informing us that it still remains in the territories of Milan.

Of this so threatening a distemper, the famous Dr. Ramazzini,[1] according to his yearly custom, on November 9, 1711, made a particular dissertation in which he inquired into the causes of the distemper

---

[1]Probably, the Italian physician Bernardino Ramazzini (1633–1714), a pioneer in occupational health with an interest in epidemic diseases in humans and animals.

From "An Extract from the *Acta Eruditorum* for the Month of March, 1713," in *Philosophical Transactions* 29 (1714–1716): 46–49.

and showed what remedies might be used to put a stop to its violent course.

It is sufficiently evident that this distemper, in the cowkind, was a true fever, from the coldness, rigor, and standing up of the hair of the cattle at first, which was soon succeeded by a violent sharp burning, with a quick pulse. That this fever was malignant, mortal, and pestilential, its concomitant symptoms plainly showed, such as great uneasiness with difficulty of breathing, great pantings with a sort of snorting, and at the beginning a kind of stupor and drowziness, a continual flux of a strong smelling matter from the nose and mouth, a very fetid dung, sometimes with blood, all rumination ceasing, pustules breaking out over the whole body on the fifth or sixth day, like the smallpox; they all generally died about the fifth or seventh day, very few of them escaping.

The author deduces this distemper from a contagious original. He tells us, it is certain, that out of a great drove, such as the merchants bring yearly into Italy out of Dalmatia and the bordering countries, one beast happened to straggle from the rest, and be left behind, which a cowherd finding, brought to a farm belonging to the illustrious and Reverend Count Borromeo, Canon of Padua. This beast infected all the cows and oxen of the place where he was taken in, with the same distemper he labored under, the beast itself dying in a few days, as did all the rest, except one only, who had a rowel,[2] put into his neck.

'Tis no strange thing therefore, if from the effluvia, like an atmosphere, proceeding from the sick cattle, from those dead, and from the cowhouses and pastures where they were fed, and by that means infected, and chiefly from the clothes of the cowherds themselves, this infection falling upon a proper subject, should diffuse itself so largely. When therefore this subtile venomous exhalation happens to meet with any of the cowkind, joining itself with the serous juices and the animal spirits, while it is carried all over the body, disorders the natural consistence of the blood, and corrupts the ferments of the viscera, whence it naturally follows, that the natural functions of the viscera are vitiated, and the requisite secretions stopped.

Dr. Ramazzini not only supposes, but asserts, that this poison is of that kind which rather fixes and coagulates, than dissolves the blood. For besides the forementioned symptoms accompanying the disease, the eye itself is a witness, since the dead carcases being opened while they are yet hot, little or no blood nevertheless runs out, those animals

---

[2]A type of spur with a wheel and sharp points off it, normally used for horses.

having naturally a thick blood, especially when the fever has continued so many days. Whether therefore this plague came first from the foreign beast, or any other way, it is the same thing, when at last it fell upon some animal in which there was the morbid seminary or ground prepared for it.

In the dead bodies of all the cattle it was particularly observed that in the omasus, or paunch, there was found a hard compact body, firmly adhering to the coats of the ventricle, of a large bulk and an intolerable smell. In other parts, as in the brain, lungs, etc., were several hydatides[3] and large bladders filled only with wind, which being opened gave a deadly stink; there were also ulcers at the root of the tongue, and bladders filled with a serum on the sides of it. This hard and compact body, like chalk, in the omasus, the author takes to be the first product of the contagious miasma. He adds a prognostic, believing that from so many attempts and experiments, and the method observed in the cure of this venom, at last a true and specific remedy will be found out to extirpate the poisonous malignity wholly. He also expects some mitigation of it, from the approaching winter and north winds. He does not think this contagion can affect human bodies, since even other species of ruminating animals, symbolizing with the cowkind, are yet untouched by it, nor was the infection catched from the air, provided due care was taken in the burying the dead bodies.

As for the cure of it: From the chirurgical part he commends bleeding, burning on both sides [of] the neck with a broad red-hot iron, making holes in the ears with a round iron, and putting the root of hellebore in the hole, a rowel or seton under the chin, in the dew-laps; he also orders the tongue and palate to be often washed and rubbed with vinegar and salt.

As for the pharmaceutical part, he recommends alexipharmics and specific cordials, and from the vegetable kingdom three ounces of jesuits bark, infused in 10 or 12 pints of cordial water or small wine, to be given in 4 or 5 doses, which is to be done in the beginning of the fever, when the beast begins to be sick. From the animal, two drams of spermaceti dissolved in warm wine. From the mineral, antimonium diaphoreticum. Against worms breeding, an infusion of quicksilver, or petroleum and milk is to be given. And lastly, as to the food, drinks made with barley or wheat flower or bread, like a ptisane, fresh sweet hay made in May and macerated in fair water. In the meantime the cattle must be kept in a warm place and clothed, to keep them as much as possible from the cold air, daily making fumigations in the

[3]Cysts.

cowhouses with juniper berries, galbanum, and the like. As to prevention, he enjoins care in cleaning the stalls, and scraping the crust off from the walls; care also is to be taken of their food, that it be good, the hay and straw not spoiled by rain in the making, and judges their food ought to be but sparing; friction, rubbing, and currying, not only with the hand, but with a currycomb and brush. . . .

17

JEAN T. DESAGULIERS

Physico-Mechanical Lectures

1717

Jean T. Desaguliers (1683–1744) belonged to the first generation of Newtonians who set down a template for the new scientific person—being scientific meant a mastery of Newtonian principles and their application in technological problem solving. He was also instrumental in making Newton's Principia *accessible to a wider audience. The excerpt that follows is more an outline of what was said at his lectures than a verbatim text. It illustrates how Newton's* Principia *escaped the mathematical and metaphysical rigors that girded it, to become the stuff of textbooks and lecture courses intended for the reasonably literate—but not necessarily mathematical—listener and reader. With practical interests and capital, such men went on to build the first factories and to apply Newtonian mechanics to power technology. Three generations after Desaguliers, in 1780s Britain, we begin to see the fruits of those applications in the nascent Industrial Revolution.*

Mechanics

LECTURE I

1. Matter is what has extension and resistance, which are properties of all kinds of bodies.

From Jean T. Desaguliers, *Physico-Mechanical Lectures* (London: Bridger and Vream, 1717).

2. Besides these, gravity is a universal principle in matter; that is, all bodies tend to one another, according to the quantity of solid matter in each body. As for example: The sun attracts the earth and the earth the sun; the earth the moon, the moon the earth. And in short, all heavenly bodies have a gravitation or attraction toward one another, as is fully demonstrated by Sir Isaac Newton.

3. By the experiment of the light of the candle passing through a hole in the paper was shown the law of that gravity, or general attraction, which decreases as you recede from the center of the attracting body, just as the square of the distances increases. As for example: If we were twice as far removed from the sun as we are, we should be attracted by it four times more weakly; if three times as far, the attraction would be nine times less.

Note that light, heat, and all qualities propagated from a center, every way observe the same laws.

4. There is another kind of attraction, namely, that of cohesion, which is called the electrical attraction unexcited, which is very strong when the parts of bodies touch one another, but decreases (when the parts of bodies are at any sensible distance) much faster than gravity, so as to become almost insensible then. This attraction is proved by the experiments made on the drop of oil of oranges; on the mercury, in the case where little cylinders of glass and iron lie at the bottom of it; on the red water and blood rising in small tubes, the hyperbola of tinged water rising between the two glass planes, and the mercury rising in a cleaned brass tube with a concave surface.

5. The repelling force in bodies, and the electrical attraction excited, appears from the experiments made with the large glass tube rubbed with the hand, which first attracts and then repels several (or indeed all) bodies, as appeared in the experiments made upon cork, lead, glass, iron, feathers, leaf-gold, etc. . . .

6. Bodies are compounded of several combinations of the first solid particles of matter; those bodies that have most compositions, having least matter, or most vacuity. Each composition affording new pores, larger than those of the last composition before.

LECTURE II

1. Motion is the force by which a body continually changes its place. The quantity of it is known by multiplying the quantity of matter into the velocity, so that a little body may have as much motion as a great one, if it has as much more velocity as it has less matter. The thing was proved by a spring shooting forward two unequal leads with the same force.

2. A down feather and a guinea fall equally fast in a glass from which the air is drawn; from this, and the former experiment may be deduced, that gravity towards the earth (or the force by which bodies fall) is always equal to the quantity of matter in bodies. Whence it follows that if two equal bodies (as the cube of iron, and that of wood) weigh unequally, there must be vacuities interspersed in that which weighs least.

3. Another proof of a vacuum is thus deduced from the last experiment. Mercury weighs 14 times more than water, and accordingly it resists to a body moving in it, 14 times more than water. . . .

Water weighs and resists 850 times more than air, whence it follows that the resistance of a medium is proportionable to its quantity of matter. Therefore, as the feather falling in the exhausted receiver meets with no sensible resistance, as it does when it falls in the air, there must be no sensible quantity of matter in the said receiver, and consequently a vacuity must be interspersed all over it. If all the world was full of matter, though never so subtle, bodies moving in such a fluid would be more resisted than if they moved in quick-silver.

4. The *materia subtilis*[1] (according to the Cartesians) impels heavy bodies downwards; therefore it must have resistance, but it makes no resistance in the exhausted receiver, therefore it is not there. If there was any matter without resistance, it would no longer be matter. Its being divided into fine parts not taking away the resistance, for a pound of gold weighs as much when in dust, as in a solid lump. . . .

6. The whole effect of mechanical engines, to sustain great weights with a small power, is produced by diminishing the velocity of the weight to be raised, and increasing that of the power in a reciprocal proportion, of the two weights, and their velocities; that is, by giving as much more velocity to the power, as it weighs. . . .

10. The center of gravity is that point by which if a body is suspended, it will remain in any given position.

11. If the center of gravity be not in the center of motion, it will descend till it goes under the center of motion, unless it be perpendicularly over it. This truth gives us a method for finding the center of gravity of the most irregular bodies by suspending them successively by different sides, and marking where a plumb-line let fall from the center of suspension touches the body in each case; observe where those lines intersect, and at that intersection the center of gravity will be.

12. The center of gravity is in the middle of a regular and homogeneous body, but not in the center of bodies that are not so, as appears

---

[1]Subtle matter; in the heavens, vortices.

from the experiments of the round piece of wood with lead on one side, and of the tobacco-pipe broken at its center of gravity and then weighed.

13. Bodies inclined cannot fall if their line of directions falls within their bases, otherwise they must fall. It is upon that principle that we keep ourselves from falling, as we walk. . . .

LECTURE III

1. The reciprocal proportion between two counter-balancing weights and their velocities holds good in all the mechanical powers.

These powers are six. 1. The balance. 2. The lever. 3. The pulley. 4. The axis in peritrochio. 5. The wedge. And 6. The screw. Though the screw being only a wedge carried round a cylinder, a great many count but five mechanical powers.

2. There are four sorts of levers. The lever of the first kind has the weight at one end, and the power at the other, with the center of motion between. The lever of the second kind has the center of motion at one end, and the power at the other, with the weight between. The lever of the third kind has the center of motion at one end, and the weight at the other, with the power between.

The lever of the fourth kind is only a bended lever of the first kind.

A compound lever is more useful than a simple one of the same length.

3. An upper pulley adds nothing to the power, but a lower one doubles its force. In compound pulleys, the above-mentioned reciprocal proportion determines their force.

4. As the circumference of the wheel to that of the axis that receives the rope, so is the force gained by an axis in peritrochio.

5. The great friction of the wedge is overcome by a smart blow. This friction is of use in the screw, which adds a vast force to the power, but raises the weight but a little way.

6. If you apply the screw (called in that case an endless screw) to the skew-teeth of a wheel, you make a compound engine of great use.

7. Let compound engines be made in any form, to know their strength, observe how much the first mover goes faster than the last mover, and so much as the effect of the engine falls short of that proportion, that is the friction.

All the mechanical powers may be reduced to the lever.

What any engine gains in strength, it loses in time.

LECTURE IV

1. The first law of motion is this. All bodies endeavor to remain in their state of rest or motion, and that is called the *vis inertia* of matter. Air resists a projectile, and gravity brings it to the ground. . . .

From this principle, a cannon-ball describes a parabola, by a mixture of the projectile force of the powder and the gravity, the whole curve being as it were made up of a great number of very small diagonals.

2. A centrifugal force is that by which any body moving in a curve (as a stone in a sling) endeavors to escape out of the curve and fly off in a right line tangent to the said curve. The string drawing to the center, and keeping the stone from flying off, shows what is meant by a centripetal force, which is just the reverse of the other.

By the centrifugal force, a whirled vessel will not spill its water, because the gravity of it is less than that force.

LECTURE V

1. The second law of motion is that the change, increase, or dimunition of motion is as the force impressed, and the direction of that force.

2. The acceleration of bodies in their fall is owing to gravity and the first law of motion. Gravity gives the motion downwards at first; the first law continues it, and gravity still superadds, till the resistance of the air is equal to what gravity is able to superadd; then the motion becomes uniform, without any more acceleration.

3. The more a body is specifically light, the sooner it comes to that uniform motion. Cork immediately comes to it, but lead is a great while first, and the bigger the lump of lead is, the longer it falls before it comes to this uniform motion, because its weight then bears a great proportion to its surface, the resistance of the air depending upon the latter.

4. The spaces which bodies fall through are as the squares of the times, as is shown by Galileo's scheme of triangles, where you see that if a body falls one space (or 16 feet and one inch in a second of time) it will fall four spaces in 2 seconds, 9 in 3, 16 in four, etc.

5. Where there is no air, bodies always accelerate their motion, in the above given proportion.

Hence it is that comets and planets in their ellipses move from the aphelion (or greatest distance from the sun) to the perihelion (or nearest distance from the sun) with an accelerated motion, and from the perihelion to the aphelion, with a motion uniformly diminished. The attraction of the sun first accelerates the motion, by conspiring with its direction, then retards it, by drawing counter to it.

6. The reason why a planet, or comet, does not fall into the sun, when nearest to it, is that the centrifugal force increases in proportion to the square of the acquired velocity and the reason that a planet or comet does not go off and leave the sun when at its aphelion it is least attracted, is that the centrifugal force diminishes in proportion to the square of the diminished velocity.

7. The orbits of planets are almost circular, but those of comets are very long ellipses, so that they must, from the laws of gravity, move a great deal faster than planets at the aphelion, and much slower at the perihelion. And that they actually do so, is plain from observation, for a ray drawn by thought from the sun to them, they sweep through equal areas in equal times, and it has been proved, that when a body revolves about another, if it describes equal areas in equal times, it is acted upon by a centripetal force, toward that central body.

8. That the centripetal force and gravity is the same thing . . . appears from the consideration that a projectile round the earth, at the moon's distance, would move just as the moon does, except some errors in the moon's motion, which are owing to the sun's attraction, that disturbs the motion of the moon, so as to make it less regular.

Hydrostaticks

LECTURE IX

1. A fluid is a body that yields to any force impressed, and so recedes most from the greatest pressure.

2. That a fluid weighs in its own element was shown by water's weighing in water and air in air, as appeared by experiment.

3. A drop of water on a table, pressed by the finger, not only acts against the table and finger, but also spreads laterally every way.

From these propositions is deduced, first, that all the parts of fluids are heavy. Secondly, that the upper press upon the lower. Thirdly, that the higher the fluid is, the more the bottom of the vessel is pressed with it. Fourthly, that the pressure of the fluid, against any part of the side of the vessel, is according to the height of the fluid above that part. Fifthly, that all the parts of a homogeneous fluid are at rest, each part being as low as it can be. Sixthly, that not only the upper surface but every imaginary surface (or surface supposed in any part, of a vessel) must be equally pressed in all its parts, which makes the upper surface be always level, because otherwise an imaginary surface in the fluid would be unequally pressed, but the parts more pressed than the rest must yield and sink down, and the parts less pressed than the rest be forced upwards. . . .

LECTURE XIV

1. That the spring of the air is equal to its weight is shown by the experiment of the mercury raised in the open tube screwed into a bottle, when by exhausting the air-pump-receiver, the spring of the air in the bottle forced up the mercury from the bottom of the bottle into the tube to as great a height as it stands in the barometer.

The other experiments upon the air-pump (which are described at large in the little book written by the maker of the pump, that gives the description of it) show,

First, that there is air in our flesh and in all liquors.

Secondly, that the air near the earth is capable of a very great expansion.

Thirdly, that air is the vehicle of sound, the sound ceasing where there is no air.

Fourthly, that air is the food of common fire.

Fifthly, that phosphorus and electrical light is helped by the absence of air.

Sixthly, that air is not necessary for the ascent of liquors in small tubes.

Seventhly, that the resistance of the air is the cause of the explosion of gunpowder, which only fires corn by corn, in a vacuum.

Eighthly, that what was attributed to nature's abhorrence of a vacuum is only owing to the air's pressure, a syringe not sucking up liquors *in vacuo*, and exhausted hemispheres, or polished plates of marble (which stuck together in the open air) dropping asunder *in vacuo.*

18

BENJAMIN FRANKLIN

Experiments and Observations on Electricity Made at Philadelphia in America

1751

Benjamin Franklin (1706–1790) proudly published the results of his Experiments and Observations on Electricity in London, taking care to note in the title that this was original experimental work done in America. Franklin borrowed from experiments made by the Dutch Newtonian Pieter van Musschenbroek (1692–1761), who is credited with inventing the glass jar, known as the Leyden jar, that could store electricity. Previously, experimenters had generated sparks but had been unable to retain the charge. Accepting that electricity is a physical entity, Franklin proved that it is a constant with equal amounts "lost" or gained, which he expresses by the notion of pluses or minuses. Here Franklin is putting in place one of the most basic concepts in the study of electricity, the notion of plus or minus charges. The book made him internationally famous and ultimately made possible the invention, in 1752, of the first protective lightning rod, the first truly practical result of electrical research. It was one of many inventions for which Franklin rightly took credit.

Letter I from Mr. Benj. Franklin, in Philadelphia, to Mr. Peter Collinson, F.R.S. London, July 28, 1747

I cannot forbear adding a few observations on M. Musschenbroek's wonderful bottle....

1. The non-electric contained in the bottle differs when electrified from a non-electric electrified out of the bottle, in this: that the electrical fire of the latter is accumulated on its surface, and forms an electrical atmosphere round it of considerable extent, but the electrical fire is crowded into the substance of the former, the glass confining it.

From Benjamin Franklin, *Experiments and Observations on Electricity Made at Philadelphia in America* (London: E. Cave, 1751).

2. At the same time that the wire and top of the bottom, etc., is electrified positively or plus, the bottom of the bottle is electrified negatively or minus, in exact proportion, i.e. whatever quantity of electrical fire is thrown in at top, an equal quantity goes out of the bottom. To understand this, suppose the common quantity of electricity in each part of the bottle, before the operation begins, is equal to 20, and at every stroke of the tube, suppose a quantity equal to 1 is thrown in; then, after the first stroke, the quantity contained in the wire and upper part of the bottle will be 21, in the bottom 19. After the second, the upper part will have 22, the lower 18, and so on till after 20 strokes, the upper part will have a quantity of electrical fire equal to 40, the lower part none, and then the operation ends, for no more can be thrown into the upper part, when no more can be driven out of the lower part. If you attempt to throw more in, it is spewed back through the wire, or flies out in loud cracks through the sides of the bottle.

3. The equilibrium cannot be restored in the bottle by inward communication or contact of the parts, but it must be done by a communication formed without the bottle, between the top and bottom, by some non-electric, touching both at the same time, in which case it is restored with a violence and quickness inexpressible: or, touching each alternately, in which case the equilibrium is restored by degrees.

4. As no more electrical fire can be thrown into the top of the bottle, when all is driven out of the bottom, so in a bottle not yet electrified, none can be thrown into the top, when none can get out at the bottom, which happens either when the bottom is too thick, or when the bottle is placed on an electric per se. Again, when the bottle is electrified, but little of the electrical fire can be drawn out from the top, by touching the wire, unless an equal quantity can at the same time get in at the bottom. Thus, place an electrified bottle on clean glass or dry wax, and you will not, by touching the wire, get out the fire from the top. Place it on a non-electric, and touch the wire, you will get it out in a short time, but soonest when you form a direct communication as above.

So wonderfully are these two states of electricity, the plus and minus, combined and balanced in this miraculous bottle! situated and related to each other in a manner that I can by no means comprehend! If it were possible that a bottle should in one part contain a quantity of air strongly compressed, and in another part a perfect vacuum, we know the equilibrium would be instantly restored within. But here we have a bottle containing at the same time a plenum of electrical fire, and a vacuum of the same fire, and yet the equilibrium cannot be restored between them but by a communication without! though the plenum presses violently to expand, and the hungry vacuum seems to attract as violently in order to be filled.

5. The shock to the nerves (or convulsion rather) is occasioned by the sudden passing of the fire through the body in its way from the top to the bottom of the bottle. The fire takes the shortest course, as Mr. Watson justly observed. But it does not appear, from experiment, that, in order for a person to be shocked, a communication with the floor is necessary, for he that holds the bottle with one hand, and touches the wire with the other, will be shocked as much, though his shoes be dry, or even standing on wax, as otherwise. And on the touch of the wire (or of the gun-barrel, which is the same thing) the fire does not proceed from the touching finger to the wire, as is supposed, but from the wire to the finger, and passes through the body to the other hand, and so into the bottom of the bottle.

Experiments Confirming the Above

EXPERIMENT I

Place an electrified phial[1] on wax, a small cork-ball suspended by a dry silk-thread held in your hand, and brought near to the wire, will first be attracted, and then repelled. When in this state of repellency, sink your hand, that the ball may be brought toward the bottom of the bottle; it will there be instantly and strongly attracted, till it has parted with its fire.

If the bottle had an electrical atmosphere, as well as the wire, an electrified cork would be repelled from one as well as from the other.

EXPERIMENT II

From the bent wire sticking in the table, let a small linen thread hang down within half an inch of the electrified phial. Touch the wire of the phial repeatedly with your finger, and at every touch you will see the thread instantly attracted by the bottle. (This is best done by a vinegar cruet, or some such bellied bottle.) As soon as you draw any fire out from the upper part by touching the wire, the lower part of the bottle draws an equal quantity in by the thread.

---

[1] Vial.

EXPERIMENT III

Fix a wire in the lead, with which the bottom of the bottle is armed, so as that bending upward its ring-end may be level with the top or ring-end of the wire in the cork and at three or four inches distance. Then electricize the bottle, and place it on wax. If a cork suspended by a silk thread hang between these two wires, it will play incessantly from one to the other, 'till the bottle is no longer electrified; that is, it fetches and carries fire from the top to the bottom of the bottle, 'till the equilibrium is restored.

A Chronology of the Scientific Revolution (1514–1752)

1514 The heliocentric theory of Nicolaus Copernicus first appears in a private manuscript known as the *Commentariolus* (The Little Commentary).

1540 Georg Joachim Rheticus, a student and friend of Copernicus and the presumed author of the first account of the heliocentric hypothesis, provides an account of the heliocentric hypothesis.

1543 Copernicus's heliocentric theory appears in his *De Revolutionibus orbium coelestium* (On the Revolutions of the Heavenly Orbs), published the year he died.

1572 "Tycho's Star" or the "Star of 1572" becomes a dramatic supernova, shocking Europe because it defies Aristotelian theory. Tycho Brahe publishes *De nova stella* (Of the New Star) the following year.

1576 Construction begins on the observatory made famous by Brahe, Uraniborg, the "Fortress of the Heavens," on the Danish island of Hven.

1577 The "Comet of 1577" made famous by Brahe also challenges Aristotelian theories.

1596 In his first publication in astronomy, *Cosmographic Mystery*, Johannes Kepler presents a Copernican worldview and draws together mathematical astronomy, physics, and a quasi-Pythagorean religious perspective in hopes of establishing a new astronomy.

1599 Brahe, expelled from Uraniborg by the king, moves outside Prague under the patronage of Rudolph II, emperor of the Holy Roman Empire.

1600 Giordano Bruno, an early Copernican, burned at the stake in Rome for his heretical opinions.

1601 Kepler appointed Imperial Mathematician after Brahe's death.

1604 Kepler publishes *Ad vitellioem paralipomena quibus astronomiae pars optica traditor* (The Optical Part of Astronomy) in which he argues that light rays are rectilinear, that they diminish in intensity by the inverse square of their distance as they travel from the light source.

1607 Galileo Galilei demonstrates that a projectile follows a parabolic path.

1608 The telescope (sometimes translated as "spyglass") is invented in the Netherlands; it uses a convex objective lens and a concave eyepiece.

1609 Galileo constructs his first telescope.

Kepler's *Astronomia nova* (New Astronomy) demonstrates that Mars moves in an elliptical path and proposes a quasi-magnetic power or virtue emanating from the sun as partial explanation for planetary motion.

1610 In his highly influential *Starry Messenger*, Galileo publishes his telescopic findings.

1611 Kepler's *Dioptrics* analyzes optical refraction and proposes a practical means to improve the Galilean telescope.

1616 Galileo is warned by the Inquisition not to hold or defend the Copernican hypothesis. This is known as the Injunction against Galileo.

1619 Kepler's *Harmonice mundi* (Harmonies of the World) presents his so-called Third Law, which draws attention to the relationship between the annual periods of the planets and their mean distances from the sun.

1620 English attorney and advocate of the "New Science" Francis Bacon publishes his *Novum organum*, seeking to establish a method based on observation and experimentation in opposition to Aristotle.

1623 Galileo publishes his strategic essay, *The Assayer*, arguing against Aristotle and the Scholastics and in favor of mathematical and experimental methods.

1624 French philosopher Pierre Gassendi (1592–1655), opposing Scholasticism, argues for what has been called "mitigated skepticism" whereby natural philosophy would be content with empirical methods and probable conclusions.

1626 In *New Atlantis*, Bacon presents an idealized institution of learning based on collaborative research turned to the common good.

1627 Kepler's *Rudolphine Tables*, based on Brahe's data and Kepler's laws of planetary motion, provide the most accurate astronomical tables until that time.

1628 William Harvey publishes *Anatomical Exercises on the Movement of the Heart and Blood.*

1632 Galileo's *Dialogue concerning the Two Chief World Systems* argues for a Copernican system.

1633 Galileo's trial for heresy before the Inquisition in Rome. After he renounces Copernican theory, Galileo is placed under house arrest for the remainder of his life.

1634 Kepler's *Somnium* (The Dream) published after his death, is a fanciful account of a voyage to the moon, arguably among the first pieces of science fiction writing.

1637 René Descartes publishes *Discourse on Method* in the Dutch Republic.

1644 Descartes' *Principles of Philosophy* supplies arguments for the mechanical philosophy.

1648 Oxford Philosophical Society meets for the first time.

1653 Christiaan Huygens applies the sine law of refraction to spherical lenses.

1654 Walter Charleton (1619–1707) presents atomism to the English in his highly influential work *Physiologia Epicuro-Gassendo-Charletoniana.*

1656 Huygens's pendulum clock opens the possibility of determining the equation of time directly.

1658 Huygens provides further information on his improved but still controversial pendulum clock, yielding a substantial increase in accuracy, now a matter of seconds per day.

Gassendi publishes a detailed exposition of Epicurean philosophy, which incorporates Christian elements and aspects of atomism, sometimes called Gassendi's "baptism of Epicurus."

1659 Huygens explains the changing appearances of Saturn as a result of its being surrounded by a flat, thin ring of matter.

1661 Robert Boyle, in *Sceptical Chymist*, argues for experiments against Aristotelian practitioners.

1662 Descartes' *Treatise on Man* is published posthumously and argues that human anatomy and physiology can be understood by means of mechanical principles.

The Royal Society of London is established by royal charter; it had met from 1660.

1665 The Parisian *Journal des Sçavans* is published for the first time, the first journal to feature scientific news, reviews and summaries of books, eulogies, and occasional editorials.

The *Philosophical Transactions of the Royal Society* begins publishing.

1667 The Paris Observatory is established by means of royal patronage.

1669 Isaac Newton builds his first reflecting telescope, known today as the Newtonian telescope.

1673 Huygens publishes another study of the pendulum clock *Horologium oscillatorium* (The Oscillation of Pendula).

Charles II establishes the Royal Observatory at Greenwich.

Boyle proposes in his *Experiments and Notes about the Mechanical Origin and Production of Electricity* that electrical effects can be explained by the emission and refraction of electrical effluvia.

1677 Anthony van Leeuwenhoek observes spermatozoa under a microscope.

1679 Robert Hooke (1635–1703) writes a letter asking Newton's opinion on the possibility of explaining the motions of the planets on the assumption of inertia and an attractive power from the sun.

1683 The Ashmolean Museum (Oxford) is established as the first public museum in England.

1687 Isaac Newton publishes *Mathematical Principles of Natural Philosophy*, or *Principia*.

1700 Gottfried Wilhelm Leibniz (1646–1716) establishes the Berlin Academy of Science.

1703 Newton is elected president of the Royal Society of London.

1704 Newton publishes the first edition of *Opticks*, based on work done during his days at Cambridge.

1713 William Derham's (1657–1735) *Physico-Theology*, and the second revised edition of Newton's *Principia* (containing an introduction by Roger Cotes) suggest a movement to use the findings of science as evidence for "design" and hence as evidence for the "designer."

1714 Daniel Fahrenheit invents the mercury thermometer in the Dutch Republic.

1752 Benjamin Franklin experiments with a kite and proves that lightning is electricity.

Questions for Consideration

1. Who do you think was the most important contributor to the Scientific Revolution? Why?

2. Describe the components that constituted the new science that took shape in the mid-seventeenth century.

3. How would a person of Descartes' time and after live as a Cartesian?

4. What did Galileo "see" on the moon? What enabled him to identify what he saw as real?

5. Many adherents of the new science also believed in alchemy or astrology, or both. How might a scientist have reconciled these seemingly different views?

6. Compare day-to-day — or ordinary — science in the early sixteenth century with that of the early eighteenth century.

7. Various authors you have read give justifications for why it is important to "do" science. Discuss and compare two such documents.

8. Science fiction is immensely popular today, but, as you saw when reading Huygens, it started in the seventeenth century. In what ways might science lead to science fiction?

9. In what ways could a woman participate in the Scientific Revolution?

10. What happened to science in Catholic Europe as a result of the condemnation of Galileo?

Selected Bibliography

GENERAL WORKS FOR EARLY MODERN EUROPEAN SCIENCE

Bono, James J. *The Word of God and the Languages of Man: Interpreting Nature in Early Modern Science and Medicine.* Madison: University of Wisconsin Press, 1995.

Dear, Peter Robert. *Revolutionizing the Sciences: European Knowledge and Its Ambitions, 1500–1700.* Princeton, N.J.: Princeton University Press, 2001.

———, ed. *The Scientific Enterprise in Early Modern Europe: Readings from Isis.* Chicago: University of Chicago Press, 1997.

Delbourgo, James, *A Most Amazing Scene of Wonders. Electricity and Enlightenment in Early America.* Cambridge, Mass.: Harvard University Press, 2006.

Gaukroger, Stephen. *The Emergence of a Scientific Culture: Science and the Shaping of Modernity, 1210–1685.* Oxford: Clarendon Press, 2006.

Harkness, Deborah E. *The Jewel House: Elizabethan London and the Scientific Revolution.* New Haven, Conn.: Yale University Press, 2007.

Harrison, Peter. *The Bible, Protestantism, and the Rise of Natural Science.* Cambridge: Cambridge University Press, 1998.

Hellyer, Marcus. *The Scientific Revolution: The Essential Readings.* London: Blackwell, 2003.

Huff, Toby E. *The Rise of Early Modern Science: Islam, China, and the West.* Cambridge: Cambridge University Press, 2003.

Jacob, James R. *The Scientific Revolution: Aspirations and Achievements, 1500–1700.* Amherst, N.Y.: Humanity Books, 1999.

Jacob, Margaret C. *Scientific Culture and the Making of the Industrial West.* New York: Oxford University Press, 1997.

Jones, Matthew. *The Good Life in the Scientific Revolution: Descartes, Pascal, Leibniz, and the Cultivation of Virtue.* Chicago: University of Chicago Press, 2006.

Lindberg, David C., and Robert S. Westman, eds. *Reappraisals of the Scientific Revolution.* Cambridge: Cambridge University Press, 1990.

Newman, William R. *Atoms and Alchemy: Chymistry and the Experimental Origins of the Scientific Revolution.* Chicago: University of Chicago Press, 2006.

Newman, William R., and Anthony Grafton, eds. *Secrets of Nature: Astrology and Alchemy in Early Modern Europe.* Cambridge, Mass.: MIT Press, 2001.
Osler, Margaret J., ed. *Rethinking the Scientific Revolution.* Cambridge: Cambridge University Press, 2000.
Park, Katharine, and Lorraine Daston, eds. *The Cambridge History of Science: Volume Three, Early Modern Science.* Cambridge: Cambridge University Press, 2006.
Saliba, George. *Islamic Science and the Making of the European Renaissance.* Cambridge, Mass.: MIT Press, 2007.
Shapin, Steven. *The Scientific Revolution.* Chicago: University of Chicago Press, 1996.
Westfall, Richard S. *The Construction of Modern Science: Mechanisms and Mechanics.* Cambridge: Cambridge University Press, 1997.

COPERNICUS

Danielson, Dennis Richard. *The First Copernican: Georg Joachim Rheticus and the Rise of the Copernican Revolution.* New York: Walker, 2006.
Fritscher, Bernhard, and Andreas Kuhne, eds. *Astronomy as a Model for the Sciences in Early Modern Times.* Augsburg, Germany: Rauner, 2006.
Kuhn, Thomas S. *The Copernican Revolution: Planetary Astronomy in the Development of Western Thought.* New York: Vintage, 1959.

SUAREZ

Copenhaver, Brian P., and Charles B. Schmitt. *Renaissance Philosophy.* New York: Oxford University Press, 1992.
Rutherford, Donald, ed. *The Cambridge Companion to Early Modern Philosophy.* Cambridge: Cambridge University Press, 2006.

BACON

Gaukroger, Stephen. *Francis Bacon and the Transformation of Early-Modern Philosophy.* Cambridge: Cambridge University Press, 2001.
Jardine, Lisa, and Alan Stewart. *Hostage to Fortune: The Troubled Life of Francis Bacon.* New York: Hill & Wang, 1998.

GALILEO

Edgerton, Samuel Y., Jr. *The Heritage of Giotto's Geometry: Art and Science on the Eve of the Scientific Revolution.* Ithaca, N.Y.: Cornell University Press, 1991.
Finocchiaro, Maurice A., ed. *The Galileo Affair: A Documentary History.* Berkeley: University of California Press, 1989.
Machamer, Peter, ed. *The Cambridge Companion to Galileo.* Cambridge: Cambridge University Press, 1998.

McMullin, Ernan, ed. *The Church and Galileo*. Notre Dame, Ind.: University of Notre Dame Press, 2005.
Redondi, Pietro. *Galileo Heretic*. Translated by Raymond Rosenthal. Princeton, N.J.: Princeton University Press, 1987.
Renn, Jürgen, ed. *Galileo in Context*. Cambridge: Cambridge University Press, 2001.

HARVEY

French, Roger K. *William Harvey's Natural Philosophy*. Cambridge: Cambridge University Press, 1994.
Fuchs, Thomas. *The Mechanization of the Heart: Harvey and Descartes*. Translated from the German by Marjorie Grene. Rochester, N.Y.: University of Rochester Press, 2001.

DESCARTES

Ariew, Roger. *Descartes and the Last Scholastics*. Ithaca, N.Y.: Cornell University Press, 1999.
Brown, Deborah Jean. *Descartes and the Passionate Mind*. Cambridge: Cambridge University Press, 2006.
Clarke, Desmond M. *Descartes: A Biography*. New York: Cambridge University Press, 2006.
Cottingham, John. *The Cambridge Companion to Descartes*. Cambridge: Cambridge University Press, 1992.
Garber, Daniel. *Descartes Embodied: Reading Cartesian Philosophy through Cartesian Science*. Cambridge: Cambridge University Press, 2001.
Schmaltz, Tad M., ed. *Receptions of Descartes: Cartesianism and Anti-Cartesianism in Early Modern Europe*. New York: Routledge, 2005.

BOYLE

Hunter, Michael. *Robert Boyle, 1627–91: Scrupulosity and Science*. Woodbridge, U.K.: Boydell Press, 2000.
Jacob, James R. *Robert Boyle and the English Revolution*. New York: Burt Franklin, 1977.
Sargent, Rose-Mary. *The Diffident Naturalist: Robert Boyle and the Philosophy of Experiment*. Chicago: University of Chicago Press, 1995.
Shapin, Steven, and Simon Schaffer. *Leviathan and the Air-pump: Hobbes, Boyle, and the Experimental Life*. Princeton, N.J.: Princeton University Press, 1985.

LEEUWENHOEK

Cobb, Matthew. *Generation: The Seventeenth-Century Scientists Who Unraveled the Secrets of Sex, Life, and Growth*. New York: Bloomsbury, 2006.

Palm, L. C., and H. A. M. Snelders, eds. *Antoni van Leeuwenhoek, 1632–1723: Studies on the Life and Work of the Delft Scientist Commemorating the 350th Anniversary of His Birthday.* Amsterdam: Rodopi, 1982.

Ruestow, Edward G. *The Microscope in the Dutch Republic: The Shaping of Discovery.* Cambridge: Cambridge University Press, 1996.

NEWTON

Berlinski, David. *Newton's Gift: How Sir Isaac Newton Unlocked the System of the World.* New York: Free Press, 2000.

Cohen, I. Bernard, and George E. Smith, eds. *The Cambridge Companion to Newton.* Cambridge: Cambridge University Press, 2002.

Dobbs, Betty Jo Teeter, and Margaret C. Jacob. *Newton and the Culture of Newtonianism.* Amherst, N.Y.: Humanity Books, 1998.

Gleick, James. *Isaac Newton.* New York: Pantheon, 2003.

Iliffe, Rob, Milo Keynes, and Rebekah Higgitt, eds. *Early Biographies of Isaac Newton: 1660–1885.* London: Pickering & Chatto, 2006.

Jacob, Margaret C., and Larry Stewart. *Practical Matter: Newton's Science in the Service of Industry and Empire, 1687–1851.* Cambridge, Mass.: Harvard University Press, 2004.

Janiak, Andrew. *Newton as Philosopher.* New York: Cambridge University Press, 2008.

HUYGENS

Andriesse, Cornelis Dirk. *Huygens: The Man behind the Principle.* Translated by Sally Miedema. Cambridge: Cambridge University Press, 2005.

MERIAN

Hollmann, Eckhard, ed. *Maria Sibylla Merian: The St. Petersburg Watercolours.* Berlin: Prestel, 2003.

Reitsma, Ella. *Maria Sibylla Merian & Daughters: Women of Art and Science.* Zwolle, The Netherlands: J. Paul Getty Museum/Waanders, 2005.

Todd, Kim. *Chrysalis: Maria Sibylla Merian and the Secrets of Metamorphosis.* New York: Harcourt, 2007.

ROYAL SOCIETY OF LONDON

Miles, Rogers B. *Science, Religion, and Belief: The Clerical Virtuosi of the Royal Society of London, 1663–1687.* New York: P. Lang, 1992.

DESAGULIERS

Stewart, Larry. *The Rise of Public Science: Rhetoric, Technology, and Natural Philosophy in Newtonian Britain, 1660–1750.* Cambridge: Cambridge University Press, 1992.

(See also Jacob and Stewart, above.)

FRANKLIN

Campbell, James. *Recovering Benjamin Franklin: An Exploration of a Life of Science and Service.* Chicago: Open Court, 1999.
Chaplin, Joyce E. *The First Scientific American: Benjamin Franklin and the Pursuit of Genius.* New York: Basic Books, 2006.

Index